GUIDO RAHR

FLOAT TUBE MAGIC
◆ ◆ ◆
A FLY FISHING ESCAPE

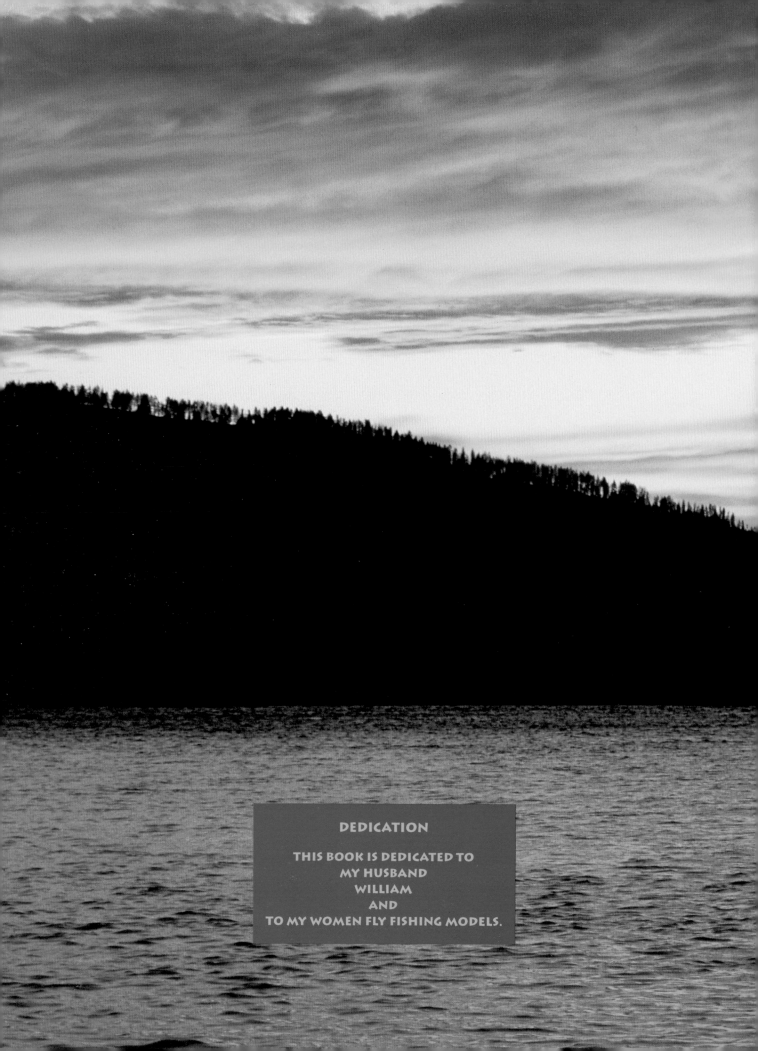

DEDICATION

THIS BOOK IS DEDICATED TO
MY HUSBAND
WILLIAM
AND
TO MY WOMEN FLY FISHING MODELS.

FLOAT TUBE MAGIC

A FLY FISHING ESCAPE

PATRICIA C. POTHIER

Frank **A**mato PORTLAND

PREFACE

This is a basic guide to float tube fly fishing for trout on western lakes using the technique of sinking lines. The reason for focusing on sinking lines is that they successfully catch fish by exploiting their day time subsurface feeding habits. In thinking about what I would include in this book, I cast back to the time when I was learning to tube fish and recalled the things I wished I had known as a novice. From this remembrance flowed the outline and content of *Float Tube Magic: A Fly Fishing Escape.*

This guide can best be used and understood if you have a degree of competence in fishing e.g., the ability to cast, assemble equipment and have an understanding of the relationship of fly fishing to aquatic animal life.

Chapter 1 introduces you to the joys you can experience in float tube fly fishing and traces the beginnings and development of this branch of fly fishing. Chapter 2 provides you with the essentials and cost to outfit yourself for float tubing. Chapter 3 is the heart of the book. It takes you step by step through the strategies of float tube fly fishing using sinking lines. Chapter 4 introduces you to the characteristics of different kinds of trout, the waters in which they live and thrive and where you are most likely to find trout on a lake.

If Chapter 3 is the heart of the book, the last two chapters on trout food might be viewed as the soul. The successful tuber needs both the strategy of Chapter 3 and the full understanding of aquatic life and artificial flies that are associated with each type of trout food which are presented in Chapters 5 and 6. These chapters provide the detailed information that is needed for a beginning float tuber to improve her or his skills. Chapter 5 describes the food that trout eat, the artificial flies that are tied to imitate these foods and when and how to fish them. Chapter 6 gives instructions for tying basic artificial lake flies.

Each of the appendices complements or adds to information in specific chapters. Appendix III on motor assisted tubing is a relatively recent development and should be of special interest to persons who because of advanced years or physical challenge, are not able to continue vigorous stream fishing or for whom float tubing without power might even be too strenuous.

GOALS AND OBJECTIVES

The major goal of this guide is to help you enjoy a successful, fulfilling float tube fly fishing experience. The objectives are that you learn:

- ◆ how to equip yourself
- ◆ how to enter and leave your tube safely
- ◆ how to fish for trout in lakes with sinking lines
- ◆ how lake fishing is affected by ecology and weather
- ◆ how to identify the most likely places to catch fish
- ◆ the kinds of food that sustain trout in lakes
- ◆ what artificial flies imitate this food source
- ◆ how these artificial flies are tied

So, read *Float Tube Magic: A Fly Fishing Escape* and then go fishing, for it is through the fishing experience that you will truly learn the art of float tube magic.
Enjoy!
Pat Pothier, 1995

ACKNOWLEDGEMENTS

Several summers ago a group of us were fishing on Mission Lake in Montana. In addition to our usual group of couples were the son and daughter of one couple who had never fly fished before. On this particular day the young people were doing very well, in fact they were outfishing some of the more experienced fishermen. In reflecting on this, one of our group said, "No wonder they are doing so well. Look at the accumulated years of fishing experience and knowledge that we have all shared with them." Yes, we all have a debt to pay and thanks to give to those who have helped us along the way.

And I wouldn't be where I am today without them.

Mentors and authors, too numerous to mention, have contributed to what I know about casting and fishing, but I do want to acknowledge those who have been especially helpful in teaching us how to float tube fly fish. First, there were Pat and John O'Neall who took Bill and I under their wing at Clark Canyon Reservoir one summer day and showed us the ropes. Our relationship and learning from these two expert fishermen continues. We were soon to find that we were not the only proteges of the O'Nealls. Among the many others were, Mike and Barbara Brickner. They in turn have extended and expanded upon the O'Neall's teaching and have shared generously with us. Two summers ago we had the distinct privilege of fishing with the legendary George Biggs. In his quiet gentle way and through his story telling he taught us many of the secrets of his success as a float tube fly fisherman. The world and fly fishing are diminished with the loss of this wise and generous man and excellent fisherman. We have also fished with Marvin Taylor who wrote one of the very first books on float tube fly fishing. He shared his expertise with us and a Taylor fly, his Little Olive Leech, which has been a winner, particularly during damselfly season.

In addition, our group of senior power-assisted tubers ranging in age from 55 to 80 years, has contributed to my growth and success as a stillwater fisher. Each person in the group has added something unique to my learning to fish. When we gather at the lakes of Montana and Idaho we make quite an armada of shared knowledge.

Then there are those who have directly contributed to the publication of this book. First, Frank Amato who agreed to publish it and made helpful suggestions. Thanks also to Kathy Johnson for her layout work and Kim Koch for fine editing. And, those who read and critiqued it thus improving each revision. The readers were of two groups: novice and expert. Since I was writing a basic book, I asked people for feedback who had not fished at all or who had not tube fished. The novices were: Eleanor O'Hanlon, Dr. Zina Mirsky, Professor Anna Shannon, Reverend Henry Bayne, Dr. Arlene and Dr. Maury Marcus. And the experts were: John O'Neall, Mike Brickner, Fred Stevens and Bill Pothier. Finally, thanks to two editors Pat Struckman and George Buice who are also in the novice category for fishing, but expert editors. Thanks all.
Pat Pothier, 1995

TABLE OF CONTENTS

◆ ◆ ◆

CHAPTER 1

INTRODUCTION TO FLOAT TUBE FLY FISHING

IS TUBING RIGHT FOR YOU?

Float tubers not infrequently catch large fish, often in beautiful serene surroundings. Best of all, they do it with an "affordable" boat in the form of a float tube that can be stored in the trunk of a car.

Perhaps you are a stream fisherman who is tired of scrambling over rocks like greased bowling balls to cast to waiting trout; walking miles up and down hot dusty trails to get to a decent fishing hole; battling dozens of other fly fishing men/women and boats for casting space on your favorite river; casting to avoid overhanging willows. If this is true for you, then it's time for you to consider stillwater fly fishing from a float tube.

Another way to decide if float tubing is for you is to imagine that you are actually having an experience of float tube fly fishing. For just a few moments place yourself in this scene:

You are sitting comfortably on a webbed seat in your float tube on the clear waters of Duck Lake just east of Glacier National Park in Montana. There are a few threatening dark clouds to the south, but just now it is clear and sunny with just a slight breeze to riffle the water. The snow-capped glacial mountains rise majestically in the west from the valley basin. This is a scene even a picture postcard cannot capture. There is a very peaceful feeling

Duck Lake, Montana, just outside Glacier National Park.

about just being able to float on the water and move about on your own power.

Paddling backward with your fins, you are slowly backing in an easterly direction, parallel with the shore. You are following a line where the shallow water drops off steeply to the next depth of the lake. You know that this is a favored feeding place for big trout. They dart from the protection of deep water, grab food from the shallows and escape to security again with a minimum amount of energy.

A trout strikes the carefully retrieved black leech imitation.

You have been casting a size eight black artificial leech with your sinking line. You let your fly slide down the drop off and then retrieve it trying to imitate the undulating movement of a leech in search of its own food. No fish have been interested in your fly for the past hour and you are lulled into inattention by the warmth of the morning sun and the beauty of the setting.

Suddenly, you wake from your dream-like state to the welcome sound of your reel singing its beautiful song as a large trout leaps through the surface film some thirty feet away. You raise your rod to set the hook. Your heart pounds. A big trout has taken your fly. You wonder if you will be able to bring it in. It jumps two more times and you see its beautiful red sides. Now, the trout is tiring

This big rainbow is finally netted after being carefully played from the reel. It will soon be gently released to grow even larger for another day's catch.

and you begin to cautiously reel it in. It is almost to your tube now, but as you reach for your net, the fish makes one more surge for freedom. You let it run, then slowly bring it to your net one final time. The trout's a beauty, perhaps four or five pounds. Carefully, you remove the hook from its jaw and suspend it gently in the water moving the fish forward and backward until it is ready to take off and return to the depths of Duck Lake.

This is an experience that every float tube fly fishing woman or man seeks and enjoys. This can be your experience.

FLOAT TUBING EVOLVES

You might wonder who invented the first float tube and why. Nobody knows for sure, but according to fishing lore, the idea for the first float tube came from a bass fisherman in Oklahoma about forty years ago and was later perfected by fly fishing men and women in the west, particularly in Idaho (Whitlock, 1992). Perhaps the inspiration for using a float tube arose when a fisherman was frustrated at not being able to reach rising fish from the shoreline and didn't want the expense and trouble of a boat. These first tubes, referred to as belly boats, were little more than an inner tube with a canvas covering and a sling seat. Contemporary tubes are covered with heavy duty nylon or vinyl coated canvas, with back and arm rests, stripping aprons to hold retrieved fly line, O rings and velcro for attaching other pieces of gear such as nets and stringers, pockets for all kinds of gear and, of course, fly boxes. And some bright person even came up with the idea of using divers swim fins for propelling the tube and to change directions, thus freeing the fly fisher to concentrate both hands on the tasks of fishing.

Some of the reasons for the interest in lake fishing are those described earlier about the advantages of lake and the disadvantages of stream fishing. An additional phenomenon that might account for the popularity of stillwater fishing from float tubes is the longevity of the vast number of people who are dedicated to the sport of fly fishing. When the spirit still wants to fish, but the aging body puts limits on capacity and endurance, lake fishing becomes a reasonable and satisfying alternative. There are women and men in their 80s who are still tubing and enjoying this unique octogenarian experience.

STILLWATER FISHING SYSTEMS

Some stillwater anglers use motor boats or prams that have the advantage of covering a lot of ground quickly but tubes allow a more careful, quiet approach to fish and have the advantage of being able to move to places that boats often cannot.

Float tubers are a diverse bunch! There are some who only use the tube to sneak quietly up to rising fish in order to cast floating lines and dry flies. Others use their floating lines only when fish are rising and most of the time use a series of sink tip (floating line with a small section in front that sinks below the surface) or sinking lines (lines which sink at a uniform rate and stay at the same level when being retrieved) to cast to fish which lie either in shallows, intermediate depths or near the bottom of lakes.

This book focuses on fly fishing with sinking lines for trout below the surface because fish feed 90 percent of the time under the water's surface and only 10 percent of the time at the surface. By concentrating fishing strategy on underwater feeding, you can take advantage of the extended period of time for fishing when there is no surface feeding. And you still have the

As dawn approaches, the float tuber experiences an early morning fog and anticipates a great day of fishing. Facing page: As the sun warms the water, the aquatic insects are stimulated to rise to the surface to fulfill their life cycle. Trout wait hungrily for their food and fishermen take advantage of their hunger.

choice of putting on a floating line at times when there is prolonged heavy surface feeding. Another compelling reason for using the sinking line approach is that success is not so dependent on sight as it is in dry fly fishing. It's more a matter of feel, detecting when a fish is taking the fly rather than watching the line and fly for movement. The flies and leaders that are used for tube fishing with sinking lines are usually larger than those used for dry fly fishing making them easier to handle for those with diminished visual or manual capacity.

A WORD ON CONSERVATION

Throughout this book you will find an emphasis on learning, on enjoyment and on preserving trout through catch and release fishing. Although each is an integral part of the experience of float tube fly fishing, the emphasis on respect for, and preservation of, trout and their environment is a critical concern. You might ask why this is true. The answer lies in the fact that there are now many more people fishing than ever before and that environmental degradation threatens the waters in which fish thrive. So, each fly fisher must be personally responsible to assure the future of excellent fly fishing for him or herself and for future generations.

First, your responsibility to the trout begins with respect for the life of the fish. This basically means what you do after you catch a fish. Do you kill it or do you handle the fish very carefully and release it back to the water to live another day. This is a decision that you must make based on certain external factors: the limit provided by regulations, your need for food or desire to eat trout and whether the fish you catch are wild trout or if they have been raised in a hatchery. Many lakes are stocked with drab colored, weak fighting hatchery raised trout. Wild trout, on the other hand, have always had to depend on themselves for survival. They are usually of brighter colors and have more native energy when hooked. Because of pollution, water diversion and increased fishing pressure,

some of these wild trout are threatened with extinction. As a result, they are often protected by no-kill or minimal limits. Since wild trout are more exciting to catch than hatchery fish, it is to the fisherman's advantage to release them to grow bigger and reproduce. So, if you choose to release the fish you catch, particularly wild trout, this action will help to assure an ample supply of fish for future generations of fly fishers and that these fish will be there for you to catch next season. Chapter 4 tells more about trout characteristics and how to identify the wild ones.

Fly fishers also need to take responsibility for the environment that supports a fishing lake. Take care not to litter the shoreline and pick up after more careless persons. Take special care to dispose of monofilament line so that it does not kill animal life that might become entangled in it. Also watch where you park your vehicle and where you walk along the shoreline so as not to disturb fragile banks and plant growth. Secondly, consider associating yourself with one of the organizations that are dedicated to conservation of the fishing environment. One such organization is Henry's Lake Foundation which has played a major role in restoring the excellence of this great trout lake in Idaho. Other conservation organizations are listed on page 43.

SUMMARY

Hopefully this introduction has peeked your interest in the joyful and satisfying sport of float tube fly fishing and helped you gain an appreciation of its origins and development from primitive beginnings to todays state of the art equipment. You know now that there are various systems of stillwater fly fishing and why this book focuses on fishing with sinking lines. Finally, you are encouraged to take individual responsibility in assuring an abundant fishing future.

Now on to how to equip yourself for your first tubing experience.

CHAPTER 2

OUTFITTING YOURSELF FOR TUBING

This chapter describes the basic equipment and protective clothing that you need to start on your float tube fly fishing adventure. If you do not have a fly fishing shop or outfitter near, you can order the recommended equipment from one of the many fishing and outfitting catalogues that are available. A partial listing of catalogues can be found under "Resources" on page 43.

BASIC EQUIPMENT

FLOAT TUBES

Your most important piece of equipment is the tube that you use to get to where you want to fish. There are now three

The traditional round-shaped tube is the most popular variation of float tube.

basic types of tubes for you to consider: round, U-shaped and power. First, the traditional round tube ($150-200) comes with back rest (which is usually an encased smaller, folded up inflated

The U-shaped tube allows for easy access and exit, especially for fishermen who are limited physically.

inner tube), mesh seat, quick release buckle, pockets, O-rings and velcro for attaching and securing equipment, a full front mesh stripping apron that stores retrieved fly line and lets water pass through. The float tube should be big enough to fit your body comfortably and yet give support to your back and legs while providing for a fairly high ride on the water's surface. Another version of the round tube is a bladder tube which is a light weight water proof ring ($150-200) without inner tubes. It can be inflated by mouth and is ideal for back packing and fishing small lakes or ponds. The newer, more expensive U-shaped tube ($275) has all the features as described above. However, it has an open front-end construction which allows more maneuverability and is easier to get in and out of. This tube is particularly useful for the physically challenged fisherman.

The motor assisted tube (POW-R Tube™ $550) has the essential features of the round tube. In addition, it has an electrical connection to a smaller tube which is zipped into the basic tube. This tube holds a 12 volt 10 amp marine battery and a small trolling motor which extends below the water line. The smaller tube is easily zipped into the covering of the larger tube.

The power assisted tube allows the fisherman to cover more water with less fatigue, to fish in heavy winds and to offer more variation in speed of retrieve.

It has a hand operated forward/reverse and speed control mounted on the left/front side of the main tube. Although the motor assisted tube is more expensive than the other types, it is much less expensive than a boat and more easily carried. The motor assisted tube allows the fly fisher to cover more water with less fatigue, fish more effectively in the wind and come back to the launching site safely and easily even against strong winds. Appendix III provides more information about this innovative, effective method of float tube fly fishing.

Usually tubes are not inflated at the time of purchase, so before taking off for a lake you need to make sure that your tubes (large and auxiliary in back rest) are inflated sufficiently to support your weight, but not enough to overstretch the seams of the fabric cover. Most gasoline service stations have compressed air and will offer this service to you. It is also a good idea to carry a portable pump and deflating tool in your car to increase or decrease the amount of air pressure due to changes in temperature or altitude. Never leave a fully inflated tube in a hot vehicle because it could explode with increased air pressure. If you need to leave it in your vehicle, release some air to prevent damage to your tube. Foot pumps are available for around $25 and air pumps that work from your automobile cigarette lighter range from $30-50.

FINS

Hard rubber or plastic fins are used by float tubers to propel themselves through the water. There are many types of fins ($30-100) used for float tube fishing. The properties to look for are those that provide you with comfort and effectiveness. You need a fin that fits comfortably over your wader foot, sock or bootie and large enough that it does not cramp your feet and is of a weight suitable to your own size and strength. Secondly, you need a fin that will be large and shaped in such a way as to give you maximum propulsion for each stroke. A popular fin made by Force Fin ($70-100) has a curved flexible "V" shape that is extremely efficient, adjustable for foot and boot size and lightweight. Its upturned tips allows you to walk forward which is

quite an advantage. Whatever type of fins you use, even if they are billed as floating, you will also need a pair of fin tethers ($7). These are usually nylon or rubber straps that fasten around your ankle and connect to the fins to prevent loss. It is very difficult to return to shore or even continue fishing if you lose one fin!

This completely outfitted tuber is ready to put on her fins, get into her tube and take off for a fishing experience.

Fish on! Before the trout took his fly, this tuber, on Clark Canyon Reservoir, was fishing with his rod pointed down into the water while retrieving his line. He raised his rod to strike and play the trout.

ROD AND REELS

The range of offerings in rods and reels for fly fishing is incredibly wide, but the most significant factor to consider is the balance (matching) between the rod weight, the reel and weight of the line to be used. Each fly rod is made for a specific weight line or range of weight lines. The price of a graphite rod can range from $90-500 and of reels from $20-200. For lake fishing with sinking lines you will need a rod that helps you cast your line a maximum distance, against strong winds and from a low position in the water. For this type of fishing with sinking lines you will not need to pay as much attention to accuracy in casting as with dry fly fishing. Some outfitters offer a combination graphite fly rod and reel set ranging in price from $150-244 which you will find quite adequate for float tube fishing. For fishing in the strong winds often encountered in large western mountain lakes a 9 or 9 1/2 foot rod which takes an 8 or 9 weight sinking line will serve you very well. In less heavy wind and smaller lakes, you can use a 9 foot rod which takes a 6-7 weight line and in even smaller lakes you might need only an 8 1/2 foot rod matched for a 4-5 weight line.

Reels not only need sufficient capacity to hold fly line and backing, but should have a smooth drag to stop large fish. Since you will be needing at least four different types of sinking lines, depending on the depth that you intend to fish, you will need extra spools (the exchangeable inner part of the reel that holds the line) for each type of line. Some reels are so relatively inexpensive ($20) you might consider buying a reel for each line you plan to use. This means that when you want to change lines while fishing, you need only exchange the reel instead of taking the spool in and out.

SINKING LINES

To gain maximum distance in casting, it is best to purchase weight forward sinking lines ($35-40). These are lines that are constructed so that the whole line sinks at the same rate. Full sink lines are different from sink tip lines which are basically floating lines with a small sinking front section. Each line needs to have at least 100 yards of Dacron backing material ($5-10) which is attached at one end to the reel spool and on the other end to the fly line. The backing allows you to let a fish run farther than the length of your fly line and also fills up the reel so that the line can be more easily handled. In addition, the backing protects the fly line from wear and tear through being wound too tightly on the spool.

Sinking lines are available in different weights and sink rates. The thinnest line, which is constructed with the least air inside, has the fastest sink rate. The deeper you fish, the faster the line sink rate you need so that you do not have to wait so long for the line to sink to the depth you plan to fish. The major advantage of full sinking lines is that you can let the line sink to the depth where you want to fish and it will stay in the feeding zone as you retrieve.

Two of the major brands of weight forward sinking lines are made by Cortland and Scientific Anglers. These two brands use different terminology for their lines and a different range of sink rates. Appendix I shows some of the types of sinking lines offered by Scientific Anglers and Cortland, their sink rate in inches per second and the recommended depth in feet for fishing each type of line. A range of sink rates is given for each type of sinking line because lighter line weights sink slower than heavier weights. For example, an 8 weight Scientific Anglers Wet Cel II line sinks faster than a 4 weight line. Knowing the sink rate of your line enables you to cast and count down your artificial fly to the precise depth you choose to fish. If you are fishing near the bottom at 15 feet and you are using a sinking line with a sink rate of 6 inches per second, when you cast your line, your line and fly will be on the bottom in 30 seconds.

Most lake fishing is either done near the surface in the productive shallows or near the bottom of the lake. The

Intermediate, Wet Cel I or Type I line is best for the shallows and the other sinking lines are used dependent on the depth of the lake. If fishing at 10-20 feet the Wet Cel II or Type II line is used. To fish down deeper, use faster sinking lines to get the fly down where you want it more quickly.

Although these lines are quite durable you do need to protect them from damage. First, you should keep your line clean. Algae from the water coats your line while fishing and builds up through normal use. To remedy this, wash the line with a mild soap and dry with a clean cloth. You can also restore a well used line to its former condition with prepared line conditioner after you have cleaned it. In between uses store your line on the reel in a place that is not excessively hot or cold. During use avoid: stepping on the line, pinching the line between spool and frame of your reel, casting in such a way that whips the line, leaving your leader attached to the fly line when storing and allowing exposure to suntan lotion, insect repellents, etc.

In summary, for fishing large western lakes it is recommended that you use a 9-9 1/2 foot rod with 8-9 weight, weight forward sinking lines with sink rates that range from slow to extra fast. Chapter 3 will provide you with more details on when and how to use these lines.

SETTING UP EQUIPMENT

The lines and leaders are connected by a series of knots: backing to reel, backing to fly line and fly line to leader. Appendix II shows you how to tie these knots and rig your line. However, in the beginning you might want to have an expert at a fly shop or an experienced friend set up your series of lines and reels. You don't want to lose a fish because of a poorly tied knot. When setting up your lines on most reels you will have to decide whether you want your reel set up for right or left hand reeling. You have a choice of using your strongest or dominant hand for reeling or for holding the rod. There seems to be a mixed opinion about which method is most effective. You may want to reel with your dominant hand because playing big fish with the reel is so important in lake fishing.

LEADERS

The leader, which is tied to the end of the fly line, is usually made of clear monofilament nylon which is considerably less conspicuous than the heavier fly line. The leader transfers energy from the rod and fly line down to the fly and gives more freedom for the fly to move naturally. Leader material comes in spools ($2.75-2.95) of different weight with the heaviest (OX) .011 in diameter and 15 pound test (will not break with 15 pound weight). The lightest (7X) is .004 in diameter and 1.9 pound test. This monofilament leader material is used for building new leaders or replacing used sections of leader.

For lake fishing with sinking fly lines you can simply use the same weight/test leader material throughout your leader. This is called a straight leader and can be attached to the fly line with a nail knot, braided loop or no-knot eyelet (see Appendix II). With frequent changes of fly, your leader will shorten and if your leader breaks off in weeds or underwater obstructions you can replace your loss quite readily with either the braided loop or no-knot eyelet set up.

Your straight leader will usually be about as long as your rod. Both the length and weight leader will depend on the fishing conditions. You want to have a leader that is strong enough to bring in the size fish you expect to catch and perhaps weather an encounter with a heavy weed bed, while still not so heavy as

to spook the fish. Leader strategy is discussed in more detail in Chapter 3.

POCKET STUFFERS AND ATTACHMENTS

Since your tube has pockets in the back and at each arm rest, you don't need the usual fishing vest. You might want to carry a camera in a sealed plastic bag in the back pocket where it is least likely to get wet. If you really want to know how heavy the fish is that you catch, pack away a small fish scale ($7-30). One side pocket will be pretty much filled with the reels and spools of leader material that are needed for exploring the various depths of the lake and the other might be devoted to your fly boxes. When selecting fly boxes ($5-50) for lake fishing, look for fairly large boxes that will fit into your zippered pocket and which are specially designed for nymphs, wet flies and streamers and that do not rust when they get wet. Chapter 6 lists the basic flies that you need for lake fishing.

Since you will be spending a good amount of time in your tube and a fish feeding frenzy might run right through lunch hour, you might want to have a sealed plastic bag with some high energy munchies to carry you over. Although you might be tempted to bring along a flask of water, this is not such a good idea since resultant elimination is a problem for tubers and a trip to the shore when fish are feeding is to be avoided at all costs. In fact, it is a good practice to limit your fluid intake in the morning before taking off for a float tubing trip. Gum and lemon balls in the stash can ease your thirst.

Your tube pockets should be about full now, but you still have your O-rings on which to attach a few more needed pieces of equipment. Your large landing net ($20-60) on an extendable cord should be attached on the side opposite your reeling hand. In order not to harm the fish, the netting should be of soft natural material. Sometimes you may want to keep a fish because it is injured, mountable or even to eat. To keep the fish alive and fresh, you need to attach it to a stringer ($3-10) which is also attached to an O-ring. It is best to place the stringer on the side opposite the net so that the fish doesn't get entangled in the net. On your dominant hand side, you can attach a forceps and line clipper on a cord where they can be readily available, but tossed out of the way when you don't need them. Small forceps ($5-6) are very helpful in removing hooks from big fish jaws. A final piece of equipment is a thermometer ($5) on a long (30ft) line to check the temperature at different levels. This gives you better clues as to when and where fish might be feeding. By marking the line at 10 foot intervals, you can also use the line as a depth finder.

SAFETY CONSIDERATIONS

For those of you who might be concerned about water safety when using float tubes, be assured that float tubing is a safe water sport even when wind driven waves are splashing around you. The way the tubes are constructed allows you to sit low in the water for greater stability. They have a low center of gravity which prevents them from turning over. In addition, most states require a second tube or other type of floatation device to accompany the main tube. If you feel the need for even more security, you can wear an inflatable life vest ($50) around your neck. A word of precaution, however: never attempt to use a float tube in moving water because there is a danger of being overturned by the current. Although you may see some advanced float tubers fishing in rivers, it is much safer to stick to still water.

WADERS

For the part of your body that will be immersed in water, chest waders that come up to the arm pits are essential. At the beginning or end of the season and in winter, neoprene waders ($85-200) with thermal long johns under them will keep you quite comfortable. In mid-summer you might want to change to light weight denier nylon waders ($45-60) or Seal-Dry rubber waders ($40-50). What you wear under these lighter weight waders depends a great deal on the temperature of the water and on your own internal tolerance for cold. In summer, some folks wear shorts under their waders while others keep their thermals on all season.

If you use stocking foot waders you will also need some type of covering for your wader feet to protect from chafing the wader with the swim fin and for walking on the shore when you enter and leave the water. The simplest and probably least expensive wader foot covering is a pair of heavy wool socks large enough to fit over the wader foot. There are also various sizes and styles of neoprene booties ($20-50) which are more expensive and durable, but must be slim enough to fit into the size and shape of the fins. Some people also wear boot foot waders ($150-200) for float tubing which gives an even more solid footing, particularly on that rare occasion when you might find it necessary to walk back to your car after being blown across the lake. However, the heavier boot foot waders require more effort in using the fins for propulsion thus are more tiring. Again, these shoes must accommodate the essential fins.

JACKETS, SHIRTS, HATS

It is very important for your comfort and safety to carefully consider what you will wear for a day on the lake in your tube. Since the lake water is usually colder than the outside air and you will be sitting directly in this water for long periods of time, you need to wear warmth in layers. On rare hot sunny days, you might consider just a long sleeve cotton shirt, but even then you should carry a rain jacket and/or other protection from a sudden change in the weather. It is best to start with too many layers than too few. A water proof rain jacket ($30-200) which can do double duty as a wind break can be easily available to you in the back pocket that makes up part of your tube's backrest. This jacket should have a hood and be long enough to cover the top of your waders without interfering with the line that you strip onto the apron of your tube. Sweaters and jackets for warmth are worn under the waders, but the weather proof jacket is worn as an outer layer allowing the water to shed off you rather than into the top of your waders. Aside from the clothing that protects your upper body, you need to have some type of head covering for protection from heat, cold, wind and errant fly hooks.

SCREENS AND GLASSES

Sunscreen is a must at all times to protect your face or any other exposed skin surface from harmful cancer causing rays. Sunglasses are needed for similar reasons. First, they protect your eyes from harmful sun rays and from your hooked fly that might come sailing back at you with a sudden gust of wind. Second, polarized sunglasses assist you in seeing aquatic activity such as nymphs swimming in sub-surface water and fish movement. To make sure your glasses don't somehow end up at the bottom of the lake, do consider a tether strap that attaches to each ear piece and hangs down the back below your hat.

GLOVES

Gloves can be useful in protecting your hands from the sun or cold. For those with sun sensitive skin, a light weight cotton glove with the fingers cut out will protect the back of your hands. For cold weather fishing there are both wool ($12-15) and neoprene gloves ($17-20) with just the thumb and forefinger cut out to facilitate tying on flies.

FOR MEN ONLY

Spending several hours in a tube, floating in the middle of a lake can be a problem for men who have reduced bladder capacity, particularly from the normal enlargement of the prostate which often comes with aging. The necessity of returning frequently to shore to relieve themselves is not only a bother and tiring, but can interfere with productive periods of fishing. In addition, there may be some people who have medical conditions that are not enhanced by the suggested limitation of fluids before tubing. One simple solution to this problem is for the man to wear an external catheter which is attached to a long rubber tube which drains urine to a holding bag. The bag is strapped to the outside of the leg just below the knee. This apparatus is worn under clothes and waders and can be put in place prior to leaving for a float tube trip. This equipment is readily available at medical supply houses and the cost is minimal for the comfort that this system provides. (My husband, Bill, says, "Try it you might like it." He does.)

CHECK LIST OF EQUIPMENT AND CLOTHING

EQUIPMENT:

Float Tube
Fins and Tethers
Rod/Reels
Sinking Lines
Leaders
Flies and Fly Boxes
Net
Stringer
Clippers
Forceps
Thermometer
Scale
Air Pump and Valves
Munchies
Sun Screen
Insect Repellent
Camera in Water Proof Bag

CLOTHING:

Waders and Wader Foot Covering
Thermal Underwear
Jacket/Sweater
Hat
Sunglasses and Tether
Gloves

CHAPTER 3

FLOAT TUBE FLY FISHING STRATEGIES

GATHERING INFORMATION

Before launching your tube, you can save yourself time and increase your effectiveness by obtaining the following information from fishermen at the lake or near-by fly fishing shop:

- ◆ Depth of the lake
- ◆ Location of inlet and outlet streams
- ◆ If there are underground springs or channels
- ◆ Specific points, drop offs or weed beds that are productive for fishing
- ◆ Insect populations that are currently hatching
- ◆ Color, size and type artificial flies that fish are taking
- ◆ Kind of line retrieve that is working best
- ◆ Depth fish are taking flies
- ◆ When there is most likely to be an insect emergence/hatch

If you are able to obtain this information, you will be ready to start fishing; however, lacking these resources, you can find out by using the techniques described in this chapter.

If you ask when you should go fishing, you might get numerous semi-scientific answers to this question such as: the moon phase; certain kinds of weather; the next insect hatching cycle; or whether cows are lying down or standing. But, the answer I like best comes from an accomplished and dedicated fly fisher. My friend, Pat O'Neall says, "The best time to go fishing is when you have the time." And, she might add, "Any other activity just keeps you away from fishing." More seriously, you will find clues as to the more productive times to fish throughout this book, but if you just like to be out on the lake whether you catch fish or not, you might follow Pat's advice.

CHOOSING A LINE AND LEADER

If you don't know much about the lake or where the fish are, you will need to rig your line and leader for a searching expedition. A slow sinking line can be used to start your search, but you should also have in your tube pocket extra reels and spools rigged with an intermediate and a fast sinking line so that you can more efficiently go to either shallower or deeper water. Your choice of strength of straight leader (all one size) depends on: the clarity of the water; the presence of underwater obstruction, such as weeds and brush; the size of your fly; and the size of the fish that you are expecting to catch in this particular lake.

If the water is murky and there are many weeds, your selected fly should be a relatively large size and the fish you expect to catch are likely to be large, you would choose a stronger leader (8,10,12 lb.). For bright, calm days with clear unobstructed water, it is better to use a lighter leader size (4-6 lb.) since it is less likely to frighten fish. If you find that large fish break off this leader, then you need to use a stronger one. In this situation, the no-knot eyelet or braided loop facilitates the easy change of leaders. When fishing in shallows and water down to 10 feet with a sinking line, you can use a 9-12 foot length leader. However, if you are fishing in depths below 10 feet the leader should be shorter (6-9 feet) so that the leader does not drift upward thus carrying the fly above the depth you choose to fish.

CHOOSING AN ARTIFICIAL FLY

(Chapters 5 and 6 discuss trout food and artificial flies in detail.)

Gold Ribbed Hare's Ear.

JIM SCHOLLMEYER

Clues as to the kind of artificial fly to use can be found on the shoreline or in the air. Look under rocks and on weeds for nymphs (immature insect stage) and crustaceans (shell covered arthropod) and shucks (outer covering of an immature insect) of recently hatched mature insects and in the air or reeds for adult

This six pound brown trout has taken a number 14 Callibaetis *flashback nymph at Clark Canyon Reservoir, south of Dillon, Montana.*

insects, such as damselflies, mayflies or caddisflies, which have already emerged from the water's surface. If you see birds or adult dragon flies feeding in the shallows this might indicate the presence of nymphs or minnows. If you are still not sure what fly will work, you can use a searching or attractor fly such as: Olive, Black or Brown Woolly Worm or Woolly Bugger; Prince Nymph; Zug Bug; Hare's Ear; Marabou or Canadian Leech. A good mid-size pattern of artificial fly to search with is a number ten or twelve. Use larger artificial flies in the spring and reduce the size as the season progresses because as a rule the insects that hatch in the spring are the largest while the subsequent generations become smaller.

RIGGING YOUR LINE

(Refer to Appendix II for the knots.)

First, mount the reel securely on the butt of your rod and run your fly line from the reel through the guides, leaving about three feet beyond the rod tip to work with. Measure off 9-10 feet of leader material from its spool and attach this leader to the no-knot eyelet with a clinch knot or a loop to loop knot with a line ending in a loop. If you are not using a loop knot or a no-knot eyelet, the leader is attached to the fly line with a nail knot. Tie your searching fly to the end of the straight leader with a clinch knot, simple loop knot or turle knot. The loop or turle knot allows the fly to move more naturally at the end of the leader. It has been observed that if a small fly is tied to a large size leader with the usually recommended clinch knot, the fly is canted and does not float freely. Finally, attach the fly to the keeper at your rod base and take up any slack in the line

and leader with the reel. Now you are ready to get into your tube and begin your fishing expedition.

If you need to change lines when you are in your tube, you can quickly and easily do this by: removing the fly, reeling in the line, removing the reel or spool and replacing it with a reel or spool of the desired type line. After securely fastening the reel or spool, dip your rod and reel into the water butt end down to thread your line through the guides. By using this method you avoid the chance of breaking your rod and it is easier on your body. Since reels are made to get wet, it will not harm the reel to submerge it for this procedure.

GETTING INTO THE TUBE

Tubing is essentially a safe form of recreation, however, getting in and out of the tube can be problematic because it is possible to fall over with the tube on top of you. Although everyone tries to avoid this, most tubers have had this experience at least once. For your safety, only launch when other people are around.

You have some choices to make on the best way for you to enter your tube. It may take some trial and error before you decide what is best for you. If you have a U-shaped tube, you can place it in the water and simply back into it. For a closed round tube you can either pull it over your head or step into it. With the motor assisted tube, it is necessary to step in because with the two tubes, battery and motor it can't be lifted over your head. For those with limited mobility, the rod butt or a folding staff can be very helpful for getting in and out of the tube and a small folding chair at the shoreline may also facilitate the process.

FOOT ENTRY METHOD

1. *Darrelle Vecchio pulling on her fins.*

2. *Tightening her fin straps and tethers.*

3. *Stepping into the tube—with her toe pointed down.*

4. *As she lifts her second foot into the tube she uses the tube for balance.*

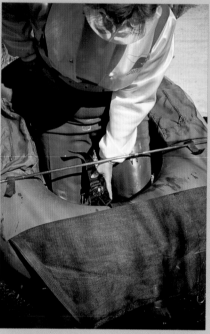

5. *Securing the safety strap on the tube.*

6. *Lifting the tube to her knees.*

7. *Turning and backing carefully into the water, avoiding rocks, logs and mud.*

8. *Floating and ready to begin kicking fins to move away from the shore.*

OVERHEAD ENTRY AND EXIT

1. The tube may be entered or exited by lifting the tube overhead.

2. To exit the tube, carefully back toward shore, again avoiding impediments.

3. Once at shore, the tube can be lifted to waist and then up and over shoulders and head.

4. Fins can also be removed before exiting the tube: undo safety strap, fin tethers and fin straps.

5. Remove fins one at a time and discard on shore.

6. Step out of tube with heel raised first, whether exiting with or without fins.

7. Rod may be used for support when lifting second foot out of tube.

CAST AND RETRIEVE

Besides locating trout in a lake, the float tuber needs to move the artificial fly in a way that simulates the movement of aquatic insects. This is done by casting the fly line and using different types of retrieve as well as altering the kicking pace.

1. Holding rod for retrieve, the line is slipped under the index finger of the hand holding the rod. The fly line is grasped between the thumb and forefinger of the retrieving hand and pulled down and back. The line is then released onto the stripping apron.

2. The coils of line are retained neatly on the apron, ready for another cast.

3. The hand twist retrieve is a very slow steady retrieve. It is executed by grasping the fly line between the thumb and forefinger, pulling a few inches of line toward the palm, rotating the wrist and recovering more line with the other fingers.

FOOT ENTRY METHOD

1. If possible choose a spot along the shore that is free of impediments or sticky mud.
2. Place assembled rod next to where you are sitting with the butt end next to you. Be careful where the tip end is resting because it is relatively fragile and easily broken.
3. Place fins on other side of where you are sitting.
4. Place tube in front of you.
5. With your feet just in the water, pull on your fins and secure the tethers.
6. Stand up in the shallow water, just to the side of the tube. Secure your balance as necessary with the rod butt or staff and step one foot at a time, toe angled down, into the tube.
7. Secure the seat safety strap and stripping apron by their respective straps.
8. Lay the rod across the tube, secure with velcro strap and with both hands lift the tube by the straps on either side to around your knees.
9. Slowly turn so that you are facing the shore and with small steps slowly walk backwards into the water, making sure there are no impediments in your way. Or you can turn sideways and side step toward the water.
10. When the water reaches your knees, sit down on the seat and you will be floating.

OVER THE HEAD ENTRY METHOD

Follow the same steps as above except instead of stepping into the tube, lift it over your head, then bring it down over your head, shoulders and waist. Again, fasten the safety belt and stripping apron and carefully back into the water.

MOVING THE TUBE

Since a great deal of float tube fly casting is done while moving in reverse, you need to start kicking backward one foot at a time once you are floating. Point the fin straight down and then bring it straight up in front of you. This motion will give you the most propulsion from your fins. Through varying the speed of your kick, you can change the pace at which you choose to fish. And, when you want to turn to the right or left, use the fins as rudders to make this change.

GETTING OUT OF THE TUBE

After you have fished as long as you want or if the weather turns inclement, it is time to head for shore. For safety, remember when venturing out that you always need to leave energy for your return. At the first sign of increase in wind velocity or the approach of stormy clouds, you need to calculate where you are and how long it will take you to paddle to safety. Since distances on the lake can be deceiving, you can help your calculation by remembering how long it took you to get to your location. It is tempting, particularly if fish are still feeding, to stay out just a little longer. Resist the temptation in favor of being on shore during a lightning storm or very strong wind.

As you approach shore, once again watch out for rocks, logs or sticky mud areas. Reel in your line, place the rod across your tube, secure with velcro straps and paddle backward into the shallows. When you can stand up, undo the stripping apron and the safety strap and walk backwards out of the water. At this point you can step out of your tube raising your heel first to facilitate egress or you can simply lift the tube up over your head. You are safely back to dry land.

For those using a power assisted tube, you may want to remove the fins before getting to shore since the tube cannot be lifted out of the water with the battery in it. In this case, once you are in shallow water, reach down to undo the fin tether, pull off your fins and throw them up on shore out of your way before stepping out of your tube.

DETERMINING WATER DEPTH AND TEMPERATURE

You can determine the depth and bottom contour of the lake off shore and the water temperature at the same time. Kick your tube out about ten feet from shore to make your first sounding. You can use an old reel filled with 30 feet of line that is knotted every ten feet with a thermometer attached to the end. Lower the thermometer to the bottom (the line will go slack when it hits the bottom) and leave it there for two minutes. Then reel it back up counting the number of knots in the return to calculate the depth and read the temperature on the thermometer. The best water temperature for trout fishing is 55-65 degrees Fahrenheit. You should also check the surface water temperature if you plan to search the shallows. Then move out to about 30 feet from the shore and repeat the procedure. If your depth sounding is between 5-15 feet keep on the number two sinking line. If the water is deeper or if you want a faster sink, use the 3 or 4 line. And, if the temperature is within the trout feeding range, you know that you don't need to go deeper to find fish as the water is in their comfort zone. Through this kind of search you can also find that productive zone where the shallows drop off into deeper water.

MOVING THE FLY

In lake fishing, there aren't the same kind of currents to move the natural insects or your artificial flies as there are in stream fishing, so your retrieve (the way you bring in line that has been cast) and speed of kick are how you impart natural movement to your artificial fly. Although this section describes various speeds of retrieve to attract fish, it is generally thought that most anglers retrieve too quickly. So, even if you are impatient to get your line in for another, perhaps better, cast, resist the temptation to go faster. A slow or super slow retrieve is often best in calm, clear water while a fast, erratic retrieve may be just the ticket on a windy, choppy day when trout are chasing insects stirred up by the wind. It is usually better, however, to err on the side of retrieving very slowly than too fast. Chapter 5 describes how the natural insects move and what is the best retrieve for each particular food source.

CAST AND RETRIEVE

After the cast, let the line sink to the selected depth and then begin to retrieve the line. The sinking line will keep the fly at this depth for most of the retrieve. To execute the retrieve, point your rod tip down the line and actually into the water, hold the rod in your dominant hand, allowing the line to slip under your index finger for control. Grasp the fly line between the thumb and forefinger of your retrieving hand and pull down and back. Then loosen your grasp on the line, letting it fall onto the stripping apron and move your hand back up the line to retrieve again. Line thus retrieved lies in coils in front of you on the stripping apron ready for your next cast. With your rod still angled toward the bottom of the lake, retrieve your line until you see the leader. Sometimes fish will follow your fly right up to the surface before taking it.

Marvin Taylor (1979) describes several useful retrieves for lake fly fishing: standard, dead drift, super quick and hand twist.

This fisherman has successfully enticed a trout to take his artificial fly by casting a fly that simulates a natural insect that the trout is interested in and by using the retrieve to lend natural movement to his fly.

TIM TOLLETT

A float tuber moves parallel to the shoreline in search of cruising trout. Trout move into these shallow waters seeking insects that live in the abundant aquatic vegetation of the shallows.

- Standard retrieve consists of three inch strips (or pulls) in groups of three with a three second pause and repeat. There are three seconds between each strip (pull-1,2,3; pull-1,2,3; pull-1,2,3; pause-1,2,3). You can vary this method by making longer strips of 8, 15 or 24 inches with the same timing of pulls and pauses.
- Dead drift is when you let the line sink to the appropriate depth and troll slowly.
- Super quick is stripping as fast as possible from bottom to surface using various length strips. This can be paired with fast kicking at the same time for even more effect.
- Hand twist is a very slow steady retrieve that is executed by grasping the fly line between the thumb and fore finger, pulling a few inches of line toward the palm, rotating the wrist and recovering even more line with the other three fingers.

Gary Borger in his excellent video, "Stillwater Fly Fishing," demonstrates a variation of these retrieves that he calls the strip tease. While stripping in the slow standard mode, vibrate the rod by moving the rod tip three inches up and down and then side to side. This added movement simulates the often erratic motion of nymphs.

Brian Farrow (1994) adds another retrieve he calls the kick-twitch-and-stop. After kicking, cast and let the line drop to the desired depth. Then instead of stripping just hold the line in your hand and manipulate it with the forefinger twitching and then pausing. With this technique your line and fly are in the water longer and you make less casts.

Gene Trump (1994) offers the turn retrieve. In the turn retrieve, you cast toward the shore, let your fly sink to the desired depth, then using your fins slowly turn your tube in a circular motion while holding your rod out. The turn allows for a smooth pulling of the fly that continues as long as you continue to rotate. This maneuver is particularly helpful in confined areas where trolling is not possible.

Another effective retrieve when fishing the bottom or into weed beds, is to lift the rod tip to the 10 o'clock position after the fly has settled, then let it drop back down by lowering your rod tip to the water. Be sure to recover any slack that may have formed in the line during this process. Slack in the line can lead to missed strikes due to the fact that you can't feel the fish take the fly. This technique can be repeated during the retrieve and is often very effective because it simulates the struggle of nymphs making their way toward the surface while still seeking the security of their previous home base.

Appendix III describes how to add to your fishing success with a motor assisted tube (POW-R Tube™). By being able to move at more speeds than is possible through fin kicking, more options for moving the fly are opened.

EXPLORATORY CASTING

Since fish usually travel around the lake in schools searching for food, your challenge is to find out where they are at a particular time. Much of the lake does not hold fish, thus you need to locate spots that are most likely to attract fish. Chapter 4 gives you more information on trout habitat to help you with your search for fish. Once you have found a likely spot, position yourself about 30 feet off shore or where your soundings indicate a drop off.

When you are ready to cast, remove the fly from the keeper and while remaining stationary, begin to work out line by false casting. You should try to cast out most of the fly line on your reel so that you will have a longer retrieve. When you are executing the false cast to let out more line, try to make your casts in a different direction from the one that you plan to fish in order not to frighten the fish. When you are ready to release the fly, turn your body in the direction you plan to fish. For example, if you are searching from left to right, you would false cast further to the left than where you plan to fish. If you have limited casting ability and want more line out, simply strip more line from your stripping apron and toss it into the water as your line is sinking. At the same time you are paying out line you need to kick backward in order to keep the line well ahead of you.

Also, in regard to casting, you need to know that sinking lines are quite heavy and cannot be easily lifted off the water especially when they have sunk to the bottom. To counteract the weighty line, you need to strip most of the line in onto the stripping apron before attempting to execute another cast.

After the cast let your fly sink down to the bottom (the line will straighten out at the end of your rod tip). Or if you know the depth from your sounding and the sink rate for your line, you can count your fly down to the bottom or to a spot just above a weed bed. For example, if the depth is 10 feet and the sink rate is 2.5 inches per second, when you count 48 seconds, you should be on the bottom. Then slowly retrieve your fly. If no fish strikes the fly at that depth, try different depths by decreasing your countdown.

FAN CASTING

From a stationary vantage point 30 feet out from shore, make casts in increments that assume the shape of a fan from your left to right facing toward the middle of the lake. Then turn facing the shore and do the same thing toward the shoreline. Using this method, you will be able to cover the water where trout are most likely to be either cruising the shallows or near the bottom around weed beds.

PARALLEL CASTING

Another exploratory method is to kick and fish parallel to the shore, staying about 30 feet out from shore. In this method, cast from a stationary position, but kick backwards when retrieving. Alternately cast directly ahead, toward the middle of the lake, or toward the shore. And, by kicking in an S pattern as you parallel the shore you can also take advantage of possible drop offs where fish might be looking for food. When fishing in a relatively small lake and casting toward shore, it is more convenient to fish counter clockwise around the lake if you are right handed and clockwise if left handed. This way you never need to cast back handed. You should also vary the speed of your kicking to see what effect that has on attracting fish to your fly.

TROLLING

Trolling is an excellent way to explore a lake. Although this method is not considered by some to be fly fishing, it is another

This fly fisher raises his arm in the back cast against a heavy wind. He will cast out almost all of his sinking line, let it sink to the desired depth and begin his retrieve. When most of the line is coiled in front of him on the stripping apron, he will lift the remaining line and leader in a back cast before he brings his arm forward to release the line. When he wants to change the direction of his cast, he manipulates the tube into a different position with his fins.

Spring wildflowers.

A friendly moose.

A rainbow after the storm.

way to find fish and it is quite relaxing. For trolling, simply cast up to 50 feet of line and let your fly sink to the depth you want without retrieving. Keep the fly moving at different speeds by adjusting your kick. If you want to fish on or near the bottom, use a line with a fast sink rate and troll at a slow speed so that the line will sink deeply and you are able to keep your fly on the bottom longer. If you are trolling for fish nearer the surface, use a slow sink rate line and a fast kick speed. Sometimes, you can be quite surprised by a big fish when trolling, so while not having to retrieve, do be prepared to strike. It is amazing how many times a fish will strike when you become distracted perhaps by watching something else or talking with a fellow fisherman. If you have tried different depths, different speeds and different types of retrieves with no fish pulling on your line, then it is time to try a different fly to see if that is the missing variable in your search for feeding fish. A good rule of thumb is to thoroughly fish a fly for 20-30 minutes before changing to another fly.

NYMPH STRATEGIES

The immature stage of aquatic insects life cycle is often referred to as a nymph and is imitated by a variety of artificial flies. Because nymphs are such an important part of the trout's diet, knowing how to most effectively fish this stage of the insect's life is important. First, you need to consider when to fish them. Trout are most interested in nymphs just before they hatch into mature insects. However, even when the peak of a particular insect hatching season is over, trout still remember and cue into nymphs. Nymphs are also available to trout as they move about in weeds and mud searching for their own food.

Exactly where the nymphs are located in a particular lake is dependent on the season and the species of insect. Usually in spring and fall nymphs are found in weedy shallows, while in summer and winter they are more likely to be around deeper

weeds. They are also found at inlets, around natural springs where the temperature never gets too hot or cold; near drop offs and mid-water shoals; and at the bottom in lakes that don't stratify.

Nymphs that are rising to the surface to emerge as mature insects are often caught in the water surface film, which is like a tight membrane. As they wait for their wings to dry and unfold they are vulnerable to trout. When trout are feeding on these trapped nymphs at the surface, you can see both their heads and tails as they scoop up this readily available food. If trout are feeding on nymphs which have not reached the water surface film you will see a bulging rise and part of the back of the fish. On observing this sub-surface feeding, use an intermediate, very slow sinking line or a floating line with a weighted fly (as described in Appendix IV). Also, if you know the direction that nymphs are traveling, cast so that your artificial fly is moving in the same direction as the nymphs. For example, the damselfly nymph must swim to shore to complete its life cycle. Trout station themselves in positions to intercept these shoreward bound insects; therefore, you must cast out toward the middle of the lake and retrieve toward the shore in the same direction that the insects are moving.

The artificial fly you use should simulate the type, color and size of the insects that are emerging. Most nymph patterns fished in mid-depths or near the bottom are fished with sinking lines. The line has a sink rate matched for the depth you are fishing, with a 6-9 foot leader and with a very slow retrieve interspersed with pauses and jerks. Chapter 5 describes specific types of nymphs and further strategies for fishing them.

WEATHER CHANGES AND STRATEGIES

Usually fly fishers consider wind to be an enemy, but for lake fishing it can mean the difference between catching and not catching fish, particularly during the summer doldrums when the trout are less active and hatches have slowed down. Wind stirs up the surface water which both oxygenates it and reduces the temperature, thus making the surface water more comfortable for insects and trout. Fish and fish food will often rise from the depths to this zone of comfort. Also, on cloudy, stormy days trout may feel less vulnerable and may be more willing to approach the surface.

The best fishing on a windy day is on the downwind shore (the direction that the wind blows toward) because insects will be blown in that direction and pile up along the shoreline. Wind currents may also stir up the weeds causing the release of insects from their safe hiding places. Surface rising fish will face the waves to catch food that is moved by the wind, so you need to angle your cast up into the wind and let your fly drift to the fish. When the fish are feeding at deeper levels on windy days cast downwind. The lower water currents run opposite the surface wave action as they bounce off the shore and cause the fish to again face into the current. You can station yourself off shore, kick backward and cast toward the shore.

While there are some advantages to a windy day, wind can also be problematic. Casting into the wind is hard work and can make it difficult to cast accurately. In addition, it can be difficult to control your line and to position yourself in a strategic place. Long rods matched for heavy weight lines (8-9) help counteract the force of the wind, along with changing casting techniques. The backcast should be snapped just past the 12 o'clock posi-

A hot non-productive August morning is followed by a windy afternoon. The author reaps the rewards that the wind brings to the trout and the fly fisher.

tion, pause for line straightening and loading and then a forceful forward movement, stopping at the 9 o'clock position for release. And, the cast should be angled toward the wind rather than directly into it. If you cast directly upwind, you will find line around your feet and in casting directly downwind you may drift right into your line.

A word of caution regarding tubing in windy weather. Waves may lap all around you and into your tube, but your tube will not sink. With rain gear you won't even get wet. The danger comes from overestimating your own stamina to kick back to shore and/or underestimating the strength of the wind. If you have concerns about your ability to kick back to your launching place, it is best to move close to shore where you can still take advantage of windy fishing opportunities. And, if you are caught in a heavy wind that you cannot handle, don't panic. You may need to let yourself be blown to shore and either walk back or wait for the wind to subside before returning to your launch site.

A float tuber rides high and dry on the waves of a windy afternoon.

Although inclement weather, particularly wind, can improve fishing, large storm systems with fluctuating barometric pressure can also turn the fishing off. Barometric pressure changes are associated with both fishing success and/or failure. With rapid barometric changes, either high or low, there is often an associated increase in insect activity and trout feeding, thus making for good fishing. However, if the barometer begins to drop slowly, you may notice in the middle of a productive hatch a sudden drop in insect activity and in fish feeding. Also, if the hatch you were expecting at 10 a.m. fails to arrive, it could also be related to weather changes. When the weather interferes with hatching and you want to continue fishing, you should switch to crustaceans, leeches and nymphs near the bottom rather than on rising insects such as emerging damsel or *Callibaetis* nymphs.

PLAYING, LANDING AND RELEASING FISH

What a wonderful feeling when a big fish takes your fly. In dry fly fishing, you can see when you have a strike as a fish takes your fly from the water surface, but in fishing with sinking lines you may not have any visual and little or no tactile warning. Since trout often take the fly softly and so far away from your rod, the first sign that you have a strike is a strong pull on your line as a trout either dives deep, takes off at a run across the lake or leaps into the air trying to throw the hook from its mouth. Since fish occasionally hit at the end of a long cast, you may wonder if a rising fish in the distance is really yours. At any sign of a fish on your line, lift the rod tip up to set the hook and then raise it high overhead to keep pressure off the leader. Through this action you can avoid having your leader broken by the strain of fighting a big fish and you are also able to keep slack out of the line. At the same time quickly reel in any slack line. You want to keep a steady pressure on the fish, but not so much that the fish breaks the leader or straightens the hook. Don't hurry the fish, let it run when it tugs, but keep a taut line. Let line off the reel when the fish surges and reel line in when the fish stops or slows down. Let the fish tire itself.

Sometimes, instead of running away from you, a trout will speed toward your tube. In this case, you must strip in line as

1. Barbara Brickner has a trout on her line. She lifts the rod to strike the fish.

2. She plays the fish from her reel, keeping the rod high and the line taut.

4. As the fish loses energy, she reels it in.

5. When it is close enough to the tube she nets it.

6. She quickly photographs it.

8. The hook is removed.

9. The fish is released.

RELEASING FISH

3. She lets the fish run when it surges.

7. Her husband, Mike, weighs it.

10. The author supports an exhausted trout until it regains enough energy to swim away.

fast as possible onto the stripping apron and then take it up with the reel as soon as possible, so that you can continue playing the fish from the tension that you put on the line with your reel. If you handle the fish efficiently during the play and through the release, there is a 95 percent chance that it will survive when you release it. Recent studies indicate that there is a direct ratio of survival to the amount of time the fish is out of water (*Trout Unlimited*, 1994).

When the trout is tired and you are able to reel it right next to the tube, hold the rod up with your dominant hand, reach for the net with your dipping hand and by moving the rod, try to get the fish to swim into the net. Once the fish is in the net, you can lay your rod across the tube, secured with velcro straps and you are ready to remove the hook. Try to keep the fish in water as much as possible and use wet hands if you must touch it. This avoids damaging the mucous film that covers the trout's body. Gently grip the fish by the tail or jaw with one hand, being careful not to squeeze it or touch the fragile gills, while removing the hook with the other. Needle nose forceps attached to the tube near your hand, can help you more readily remove deeply hooked flies. If the hook is too hard to remove, cut the leader and nature will heal what is left. After the hook is out and while the fish is still in the net, is the time to weigh and measure your fish using the scale from your tube pocket and a marking measure which is on the front of most tube aprons. If you choose to take photographs before releasing your fish, set up the photo before removing the fish from the water. Again, gently support its body just above the water, being careful to keep your fingers away from its gills. Occasionally, you may get a trophy fish that is appropriate for mounting, but at the same time you feel reluctant to kill such a marvelous trout. If you thoroughly photograph, measure and weigh your fish, a taxidermist can reconstruct your treasured catch.

To release the fish, hold it firmly by the tail so that the fish's back is upright in the water and provide gentle support under the fish just behind the head. Move the fish back and forth to help the gills begin pumping oxygen and to help the fish rest and regain its strength. If the fish turns "belly up" when you release it, retrieve it and continue to support it until it can swim away on its own strength.

SERENDIPITY

In spite of following all these recommended methods and strategies, sometimes you simply don't catch fish. Even when you are right next to another person who is catching fish and doing just what that person is doing, you may not catch fish. This is very frustrating for the person not catching fish, but for the one catching fish it is pure joy. But, as fishing goes, what goes around comes around. So, when you are catching you can be most grateful and if you are not you can wait for a better day.

It helps to keep records of your fishing, not just what was caught and when, but the conditions under which you were successful: water temperature; depth; retrieve; type, color, size fly; weather conditions/barometric pressure; and where on the lake you found fish. Remembering a weed bed, channel or drop off may be somewhat difficult, but if you triangulate your sites with permanent shoreline objects and record this data in your fishing diary, you will be able to find these spots in the future.

A final word of advice. There is no right or wrong way to fish. Try different methods and be creative. Be courageous, even consider doing the outrageous some day and see what happens.

CHAPTER 4

TROUT AND THEIR HABITAT

Since one of the major goals of fly fishing is catching trout, you will want to know more about their habitat and how to identify them when you make a successful catch. First, trout belong to a group of salmonoid fish which includes: salmon, trout, smelt and whitefish. They are streamlined with well developed dorsal and adipose fins. Hatchery trout can be distinguished from wild trout by examining these fins. The smooth adipose fin, located toward the rear of the back may be clipped off in hatchery fish and the large rayed dorsal fin more toward the front of the back may be bent, crooked or clipped off. Some hatchery bred fish are sterile. These fish often grow faster and larger than fertile fish because they do not need to expend energy in reproduction.

Brook trout.

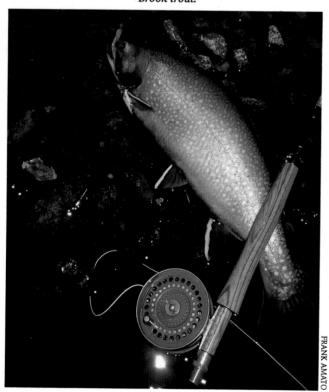

FRANK AMATO

Unlike trout which live in streams and wait for food to come to them, lake trout must travel around the lake in search of its food. They usually travel in schools looking for food sources while at the same time watching out for predators. Fortunately, they have a highly developed sensory system which helps them locate food and protects them from danger.

The trout that you are most likely to encounter in western lakes are strains of: brook *(Salvelinus fontinalis)*, brown *(Salmo trutta)*, cutthroat *(Salmo clarki)* and rainbow *(Salmo gairdneri)*.

BROOK TROUT

Brook trout are native to the northeastern region of America. From there they were introduced into many other regions. They are distinguished by: red spots with blue aureoles on the sides of the fish; dark wavy lines on the back and dorsal fin; pink or reddish lower fins edged with white; and square tails. Although larger brook trout have been caught, a five pound brook is exceptional. The reason that they do not grow larger is because they have a relatively short life span, usually under four years.

Brook trout require colder water than other species of trout. They thrive in water less than 65 degrees F and the upper limit for survival is 75 degrees F. In addition, brook trout require water with specific chemical and physical properties in order to thrive. Henry's Lake in Idaho supports a healthy brook trout population.

BROWN TROUT

The brown is a native of Europe and was introduced to North America in the late 1800s. It is known to be quite hardy and resistant to environmental changes. But, it doesn't tolerate water that is less aerated or of higher temperatures. Compared with brook and rainbow trout, the brown is often considered wary and more difficult to catch, particularly the larger browns. For these reasons, some brown trout grow to be quite large.

The brown trout is a golden brown color with large brown or black spots on its sides, back and dorsal fins. Spots may be circled by halos of a lighter shade than the body and a few red or orange spots appear on lateral surfaces and adipose fin. The belly is usually yellow to creamy in color and the tail is almost square.

Rainbow trout.

Although browns forage for food, such as hatching insects, during the day, they are known to be very active night feeders. Some of the largest brown trout are caught in the evening after dusk. Mature browns are also known for their predation on young trout and other aquatic animals. When caught, browns tend to drop or dive toward the bottom of the lake and are resistant to being moved from that position. Browns tend to put up a good fight, which resembles a tug of war, in contrast to the acrobatic rainbows.

CUTTHROAT TROUT

The cutthroat is a native of the intermountain west and wild populations are common in Montana, Wyoming and Idaho. Its life span is about six years and a good maximum size is five pounds. Its name comes from the characteristic red slash below the jaw. The body colors vary with sub-species from yellowish-green to rainbow colors. It may have red on the side of the head with numerous dark spots over its body. When caught, the cutthroat is not as active as the rainbow, seldom jumping. It has a reputation for being relatively easy to catch.

Cutthroat trout.

RAINBOW TROUT

These natives of the west are the most sought after of trout species because of their fighting characteristics and potential size. They are the acrobats of fly fishing with their jumps and runs. They have been exported all over the world because of these characteristics and because they are very adaptable to dif-

Brown trout.

ferent bodies of water. Unlike brown trout, which require cold well aerated water, rainbows will tolerate somewhat warmer and less aerated conditions.

The coloring of rainbows can be quite variable depending on the sub-species or strain. The one distinguishing feature that most all rainbow trout have is a red lateral band. The back is often dark blue/green, with silver sides grading to a white belly. Rainbow trout will eat almost anything and they often feed for longer periods of time than other trout. Rainbows in food rich water can grow quite large and can make rapid growth rates, 6-7 pounds in three years.

You might also encounter hybrid trout in your lake fishing. One type of hybrid that occurs either naturally or is artificially bred is a combination of rainbow and cutthroat. If you catch a

*Large reservoirs, like Clark Canyon, are stocked with fish and have greatly
expanded lake fishing opportunities for fly fishing women and men.*

fish that has the characteristic red slash of the cutthroat but the fighting characteristics and overall appearance of a rainbow, you may have caught a hybrid trout. Hybrid fish are usually sterile.

WHERE TROUT LIVE

LAKE FORMATION AND PROPERTIES

Waters throughout the world, whether in the ocean, stream or lake have certain commonalities as well as notable differences, such as degree of salinity. The water in streams and lakes are more alike and have similar dissolved properties. A major difference between lake and stream water is that stream water moves at a pace which guarantees a constant supply of oxygen and a vehicle for carrying food sources to where trout lie in protected spots in wait for food. Lake water, on the other hand, is a reservoir for water that may come from streams, rain, snow and

*A small lake, like Mitten in Montana,
offers excellent tubing in beautiful surroundings.
However, the size and quantity of fish in this lake can be
variable because it is shallow and subject to winter fish kills.*

springs. Compared with a river, lake water seems still, but in fact lake water is in constant motion and change due to the input from tributaries, wind and seasonal ecological changes.

NATURAL LAKES

Natural lakes occur when geologic events such as volcanic activity, glaciers and earthquakes form a basin in which water collects. The water that flows into a lake greatly influences the character of the lake. A lake is called eutrophic when it is surrounded by fertile land which supplies rich nutrients to the lake. Oligotrophic lakes, on the other hand, have few nutrients and the soil surrounding them tends to be quite barren. Both types of lakes are subject to environmental contamination from pesticides and other chemicals that effect the quality of the water to support a fishery. Even eutrophic lakes can suffer from over fertilization.

RESERVOIRS

Man-made lakes, reservoirs, result from damming a river or stream. They have both an inlet and outlet as well as tributary streams feeding into it. The reason for constructing these dams can be for control of flooding, hydroelectric power and for reserving drinking and irrigation water. The reservoir tends to have fairly stable water heights, except when extreme weather conditions lead to temporary instability or when man's needs for water requires that this water be drawn upon. These reservoirs have greatly expanded lake fishing opportunities beyond what was possible from natural lakes.

QUALITIES OF A FLY FISHING LAKE

Lakes vary in size from small ponds to thousands of acres. Fly fishers tend to prefer smaller and medium size lakes or bays of larger lakes which have shallows with abundant plant growth and channels with depths to about thirty feet. Larger, deep lakes are fishable, but it is harder to find fish because there is less shore line in relation to the depth and there is often much variation from cove to cove.

In his new book, *Float Tubing the West,* published by Belly Boat Publishing, Marvin Taylor lists his favorite float tubing lakes in the west: the Clark Canyon Reservoir, Montana; Daniels Reservoir, Idaho; Henry's Lake, Idaho; Horse Thief Reservoir, Idaho; Island Park Reservoir, Idaho; Little Camas Reservoir, Idaho; Malheur Reservoir, Oregon; Mission Lake, Montana; Mitten Lake, Montana; Mountain View Reservoir, Idaho/Nevada; Pyramid Lake, Nevada; Sheep Creek Reservoir, Idaho/Nevada. You might consider exploring one of these productive lakes as you begin to learn float tube fly fishing.

LAKE MANAGEMENT

Most states have a governmental agency which manages the fisheries within its borders. Increasingly fishery management is based on a growing scientific knowledge of the needs of fish and their environment. These scientific managers decide what type of trout, and how many, a specific body of water can support. They stock the lake and set catch/bag limits accordingly. They also work on maintaining a supportive fishing environment by actions such as replanting a shore line or fencing areas against cattle. These agencies usually manage the state hatcheries which are devoted to breeding of trout by artificial means to provide angling stock. The specific strain of trout they choose to breed depends on: the quality of water that they will be transferred to; their growth rate; their desirability as a sport fish; and their ability to adapt to a new environment.

ELEMENTS OF A TROUT LAKE

A productive fishing lake must have conditions that support abundant plant, insect and trout growth. The major inter-related variables that support a productive trout lake are: sunlight, relative alkalinity, temperature and oxygen.

Mission Lake, on the Blackfeet Reservation in Montana, is famous among float tubers for the size of the trout available and for the ferocity of the winds that sweep down from Canada and the nearby Glacier Park peaks.

SUNLIGHT/ALKALINITY

Sunlight is essential to the growth of plant life through photosynthesis. With the aid of radiant energy, chemical compounds are synthesized to form carbohydrates in the chlorophyll-containing tissues of plants that are exposed to light. An important by-product of this photosynthesis process is the production of oxygen, which all living creatures need. Lakes that have a high alkaline content are more likely to have abundant plant life because they tend to be clear, which allows for deep penetration by the sun.

The degree of brightness of sunlight also affects the behavior of fish. During bright calm days, trout feel vulnerable and are

A bay, such as this one in Hebgen Lake, Montana, offers the tuber opportunities to fish without having to explore the large expanse of water in a big lake. It also offers some protection from the wind.

Legendary Henry's Lake in Idaho, is a rich eutrophic lake with extensive weed beds and a healthy population of fish. It is particularly popular during the damselfly season in June.

more likely to seek out deeper or more protected spots. When days are cloudy or when the light is low in the morning or evening, trout are also more likely to rise and feed with less concern for their safety.

TEMPERATURE

Water temperature determines when insects will rise from their aquatic habitat to the surface in order to complete their life cycle. Because trout are most comfortable and actively feed in water that is 55-65 degrees Fahrenheit, the water temperature also determines where trout will be found and when they will be most likely to feed.

OXYGEN

In addition to sunlight, aquatic organisms depend for their existence and growth on an adequate supply of dissolved oxygen. The amount of dissolved oxygen available to them depends on temperature, altitude, wind and plants. The quantity of dissolved oxygen increases with cooler water and lower altitudes and decreases with warmer water and higher altitudes. Fish will move away from warm water to cooler water deeper in lakes, near springs and inlets to meet their need for more oxygen. A major source of oxygen in lakes is from surface mixing with the air. Wind whips up the surface water enabling oxygen from the air to enrich the surface water. And, as previously mentioned, oxygen is released from plants into the water as a by-product of photosynthesis.

TROUT FOOD CHAIN

All organisms belong to a food chain which is an interrelated complex web with each part being dependent on another part. Plants and algae (vascular plants with chlorophyll) absorb nutrients, photosynthesize and grow. These plants are consumed by small zooplankton which are minute plant and animal life that float or swim weakly in water. The zooplankton, in turn, are consumed by larger animals such as insects, scuds and leeches. These animals become the basic elements of the trout's diet.

Shallow areas where rooted plants grow are often the most productive part of a lake because plants/algae at this depth have a maximum light source for photosynthesis. Insects gain nourishment from plankton and literally crawl out of the aquatic plants as they migrate to the surface or shore to fulfill their life cycle.

SEASONAL CHANGES IN LAKES

Because seasonal changes in lake ecology affect trout behavior and insect growth, it is helpful to know what to expect from each season on a lake. To understand how the lake changes with the seasons, it is important to remember that water is densest at 39.2 degrees Fahrenheit and that it gets lighter when it is colder or warmer. Since water freezes at 32 degrees, ice floats on the top of the denser warmer water. If water became heavier with cold, it would freeze to the bottom of the lake and kill all the fish.

Because of the cooler water and less sunlight to support photosynthesis, winter is a time of hibernation in the lake for plants, insects and fish. Trout will feed mostly on crustaceans and leeches during the winter months.

In spring, when the surface warms and the ice melts (ice out), the water layers begin to mix. Warmer water rises and mixes with surface water and the whole lake reaches a uniform 39.2 degrees. Wind facilitates circulation of the water bringing needed oxygen to deeper levels and moving essential nutrients toward the surface where they can support plant and insect growth. This is called the spring "turnover". It is a time for trout to feast on this new food source after their long restricted winter diet.

In early summer, the insects continue to hatch and trout cue into each subsequent generation of food source. By late summer, increased water temperature often causes trout to become sluggish and seek the comfort of deeper, cooler depths and around springs. In deeper lakes, summer may bring a stratification of layers of water. Wind generates surface currents causing warm surface water to slide over deeper, colder water thus making a thermocline layer which is a comfort zone between the cold poorly oxygenated depths and the warmer surface water.

Fall brings another lake "turnover". As the upper layer of the lake cools, it falls toward the bottom which brings oxygen and nutrients down with it. The whole lake again becomes a comfort zone for trout. This "turnover" brings a resurgence of plant growth and insect activity which provides trout with a rich source of food before winter stagnation sets in.

FINDING A PRODUCTIVE FISHING SPOT

Your best source of information on where to fish in a given lake is to ask either at a fly fishing shop or fishermen at the lake. You can also observe where boats or tubes are congregated on the lake. Your best observation spot may be an overlook where you have some elevation to assist your assessment of the lake. Binoculars might assist you with your observations. From this vantage point you can look for places where trout are most likely to seek food while at the same time seeking protection: weedy areas, drop offs, peninsulas, rocky outcroppings, brush and tree trunks, shoals in deeper water and inlet, outlet and tributory stream locations. You can also observe which way the wind is blowing since insects will be blown to the downwind shore where fish feed on them in the foam line.

Trout cruise the shallows in search of food or they lie in deeper water just off the shallows. From a shelf or ledge, they move easily to feed in the shallows and then back to the safety and comfort of deep, cool water. They are also found in the next

Kipp Lake, Blackfeet Reservation, Montana.

deepest area of the lake where there are floating weeds which harbor an abundance of insects. And, trout may be in even deeper water where submerged weed beds grow as far down as the light extends in the lake. These weed beds are rich in insects and scuds and also provide shelter for trout. Trout also gather at incoming or outgoing streams because currents and the aeration provide stimulation for nymph activity of which the fish take advantage. In addition to hiding under ledges trout will also seek cover under submerged logs, rocky points and overhanging foliage. Underwater springs provide trout with a comfort zone where the temperature remains constant even when other parts of the lake are too warm or cold.

SUMMARY

You are now aware of the characteristics of different kinds of trout that you are likely to encounter in western waters; the elements of a productive fishing habitat; the importance of the food chain to productive fishing; and where on a given lake you are most likely to find feeding fish. The next two chapters will provide you with more specific information about trout food, which is the basis for understanding fly fishing and descriptions of the essential artificial flies needed for successful lake fishing.

Large Lake, Mission, Montana.

CHAPTER 5

TROUT FOOD

RELATIONSHIP OF ARTIFICIALS TO NATURALS

Although strategy is often more than half the game, the right artificial fly for the situation and season is essential to successful float tube fly fishing. Some tubers have many boxes of flies in their repertoire which they have found to be successful at different times and places. In fact, they can usually tell you exactly where they fished a certain fly, what fish they caught and what the weather was like on that particular day. Other tubers tend to use a limited repertoire of flies and depend more on strategy. This chapter alphabetically lists basic trout food, the artificial flies that are connected with this food source and when and how they should be fished.

Most of the basic artificial lake flies can be found in trout shops near the western lake that you choose to fish, but some are hard to come by in a range of colors and sizes. Therefore, I strongly urge you to invest in fly tying equipment and materials and to take a beginning fly tying course. If a course is not available in your area, books and video tapes on the basics of fly tying

The caddis pupa is the most important stage for trout feeding. The pupa breaks out of its larval case and begins its rapid transit to the surface where it transforms into an adult and flies away.

Callibaetis nymphs are one of the most important mayflies for western lake fishing. They have a long productive season, but their major hatching activity is in June and July.

can help you get started. Lake flies are not hard to tie as most involve a few simple steps and fairly large sized hooks. Besides, you have more variety readily available when you tie your own flies and will learn more about each fly and its fishable qualities. Nothing beats catching a huge trout on your own hand-tied fly!

The major sources of western lake trout food are: caddis larvae and pupae; callibaetis mayfly nymphs; chironomid pupae; damsel and dragonfly nymphs; forage fish; leeches; and scud. Chapter 6 shows the materials and gives directions for tying these basic, effective artificial flies which mimic food sources. A range of colors and sizes is given for each and it should be noted that the smaller sizes are best used as the season progresses because insects, especially caddis and mayflies, become smaller with each succeeding hatch during the growing season.

Artificial flies ("artificials") that are connected to these food sources may be tied in close imitations of a specific kind of food, but more often the effective artificial is more suggestive of a

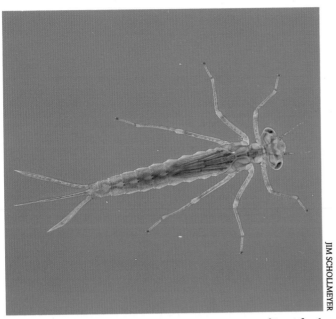

Damselfly nymphs are also a very important source of trout food. Damsels hatch several times from April to September. The hatching cycle varies from lake to lake.

food source or is an attractor. The artificials listed below each trout food source are of both types. In considering why trout take flies that are not close imitations, it is hypothesized that they are taken for reasons other than hunger, such as curiosity, convenience, natural aggression and for dietary variety (Tullis, 1992). When fishing in deeper water or on a dull day, the attractor fly is more likely to get a fish's attention than is a close imitation. Many attractor flies are made with peacock herl bodies, tinsel wraps and mylar wing cases which reflect natural iridescence and brilliance.

Aquatic insects and animals are accessible and vulnerable to trout at specific times: when they are moving about seeking their own source of food; when they are fleeing from predators; and when they are emerging to the surface or shore in order to fulfill their life cycle. It is the emergence of nymphs and pupae that is the most important part of the insect's life for both the trout and the fly fisher. Since each of these trout food sources has its own peculiar time table and movement characteristics, your goal is to have an artificial fly that you can move to simulate the natural characteristics of the trout food source.

CADDISFLY

There are numerous species and colors of caddis fly, however, each has a life cycle of: egg, larva, pupa, adult. The larvae and pupae, are the most important stages for trout feeding. The larvae may grow up to 1 inch in length and are encased in a protective covering. They are found in less than twenty feet of water around plants and rocky bottoms. Caddis pupae may be from about 1/4-1 inch long and colored with shades of browns and olives. They have roundish, soft bodies and long antennae over their backs. When the pupa breaks out of its larval case, it quickly rides to the surface in self-generated gas bubbles and at the surface the adult flies away almost immediately.

Caddis hatches are strongest in the spring to mid-summer and the time of the daily hatch can be quite variable. Although clouds of adults are often seen to be active toward late evening the pupa emergence may occur at a different time. It is helpful

to find out from local fishers when the caddis usually emerge on a particular lake so that you can fish the pupa before the fluttering adults appear in the air. The adults have wings that fold tent-like back on their bodies and the wings are usually light in color. The caddis pupa often have the same color body as the adult.

The emerging pupae, which rise straight up through the water, may be fished with an intermediate or floating line and a weighted fly. Let the fly sink and then raise the fly toward the surface with unbroken motion to simulate the caddis pupa's fast rise. The larva stage is fished with a sinking line at the bottom of the lake or into weed beds. The retrieve is slow, hand twist alternating with jerky movements.

Patterns associated with caddis larva are: Woolly Worms (brown and olive); Renegade; Halloween; Beaver and Tan (and flies tied with other shades of variegated chenille). And, for the emerging caddis pupa various Sparkle Emerger patterns.

CALLIBAETIS MAYFLY

The *Callibaetis* is by far the most important mayfly for western lake fishing. As with all mayflies, it has a four-stage life cycle: egg, nymph, adult (dun) and spinner. The emergence of this 1/2-3/4 inch long slim, agile, three-tailed nymph is most important in lake fly fishing. You might find out from local fishing sources when to expect a *Callibaetis* emergence, but lacking this resource, you will know that the hatch has begun when you see grey speckled wing adults on the water surface or in the air. Nymph colors usually reflect the protective coloring of the vegetation in which they live. Common colors are shades of brown/olive, grey/olive and greens. *Callibaetis* nymphs are found in shallow water around aquatic vegetation where they

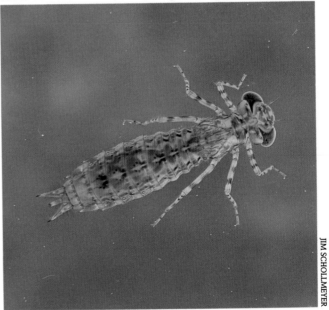

Dragonfly nymphs are similar to damsels only much larger. They are not as abundant as damsels, but still provide trout with a fine food source.

feed on plankton and algae. Prior to emergence, they are vulnerable to trout and to voracious dragonfly nymphs that also crawl around the bottom and on plants in their own search for food. When they are ready to emerge, their bodies become more buoyant because their abdomens fill with air. As they begin to move upward, they feel vulnerable and wiggle to get back to the safety of the bottom. Their emergence from the weed beds and through the surface film is a slow process which makes them particularly vulnerable to trout. *Callibaetis* nymphs are most active on sunny summer mornings starting around 9:00 a.m. and extending into the afternoon. The *Callibaetis* mayfly has a long productive season, but the major hatching activity is in June and July.

When the nymphs are moving on the bottom, fish your imitation slowly interspersed with quick jerky movements to simulate the nymph fleeing from a predator, such as a dragonfly nymph. Also to simulate the struggle of the nymph, lift the fly and then drop in a jerky movement by lifting the rod tip and then letting it drop while giving a short quick strip. At emergence, the nymph swims to the surface by undulating its tail and body back and forth with occasional rest pauses on the way. Casts should be made just over or next to weed beds and retrieved in the same direction that the nymphs are moving. To simulate the nymphal movement your retrieve should be a very slow standard retrieve. Since the nymph emerges relatively slowly from the surface film, you should use a floating or intermediate line as described in Appendix IV. When the nymphs are emerging near the surface, make long steady pulls to bring up your artificial. Patterns associated with the *Callibaetis* mayfly nymph are: Hare's Ear Nymph (Gold Ribbed, Flashback or Plain); *Callibaetis* Nymph (Plain or Flashback); Pheasant Tail Nymph (Flashback or Plain); Peacock Nymph; Zug Bug; Prince Nymph; Biggs Fly (Sheep Creek).

CHIRONOMID

Unlike most lake insects, chironomid/midge are usually quite small but what they lack in size they more than make up in numbers. There are countless varieties of these insects and they are found in almost any location in the lake. Midges are usually tiny, 1/4 inch or less. They have four life stages: egg, larvae, pupae and adult. The most important life stage for trout feeding is when the pupae are slowly moving toward the surface. They are found in areas of rich plant life throughout the lake and they hatch all season with the peak being June and July.

Chironomid, or midges, are small, but the most abundant insect for trout food. The most important life stage for trout feeding is when the pupae slowly move toward the surface and are often caught in the surface film where they are easy prey for trout.

Chironomid pupae have thin segmented abdomens with a thick thorax and tufted gills at the head. The pupae colors vary with the type of chironomid and vegetation in which they live. Usual color variations are grey, tan, brown, cream, olive, amber and black. The pupa may be the same color as the body of the emerging adult. The adult chironomid has long legs and a body that is longer than its wings. The bodies are slightly humped and may have a segmented striped look.

JIM SCHOLLMEYER

Scud are a major source of trout food all year and are prevalent in all lakes, particularly where the water has high alkalinity and oxygen.

Chironomid hatches can occur at any time. Some species emerge at sunset, others in late morning or early afternoon and there are those that hatch constantly day and night. The pupae are slow swimmers that struggle toward the surface with frequent stops for rest. They are vulnerable to trout during their ascent but particularly at the surface as they hang in the surface film until the adult breaks out and flies away.

For midge pupae and adults trapped in the surface film, use the floating line method described in Appendix IV. Use sinking lines for sub-surface insects. The retrieve should simulate the slowly swimming pupae. Only move your fly an inch or two at a time and pause between each movement. Most importantly retrieve very slowly. Patterns associated with chironomid are: TDC Midge; Tunkwanamid; Griffith's Gnat (adult).

DAMSEL AND DRAGONFLIES

These lake flies have only three stages to their life cycle: egg, nymph and adult. While there may be many adults on the surface, the most important stage for fishing is the nymph. Damsels and dragon flies hatch several times from April to September with the major hatches occuring in June and July. The hatching cycle varies from lake to lake.

DAMSELFLY NYMPHS

The beady eyed, slender damselfly nymph is 1/4-1/2 inches long, has a hinged lower jaw for grasping prey and a distinctive three bladed tail. It is colored in shades of olive, bright green, tan and brown usually blending with the color of surrounding vegetation. The nymph lives in depths down to twenty feet where it feeds on both plant and animal life. In order for the adults to emerge from their nymphal shucks, the nymphs must migrate from wherever they live in the lake toward the shore. In a large lake this could mean traveling as much as half a mile from the middle of a lake. They are most likely to migrate in large groups on sunny days late in the morning. The damsel nymph swims using a graceful side to side pollywog type movement with pauses for rest and occasional bursts of speed if frightened. Since damsel nymphs migrate toward shore, your cast should be made so that you can retrieve your fly in the same direction that the nymphs are moving. The damselfly is fished with a slow standard retrieve combined with the strip tease from the bottom to the surface. Patterns associated with damselfly nymphs are: Damselfly Nymph; Little Olive Leech; Biggs Fly (Sheep Creek).

DRAGONFLY NYMPHS

Dragon fly nymphs, while not as abundant as damsels, are also significant trout food. They are larger and bulkier than damsels with an average length of 1-2 inches and a distinctive hour glass shape. Their coloration tends toward greens and browns. Like damsels they also have a hinged jaw and are known for their voracious feeding both as nymphs and adults. Although they may creep along the bottom in search of food, they are more likely to remain hidden in plant growth until a smaller insect passes by and is grabbed by their strong jaws. When they are fleeing a predator, they move in a quick jerky style as they are propelled by water taken in through their mouth and expelled through their anus. Since dragonfly nymphs crawl on the bottom to their place of exit at the shore, you must fish your imitation deep using a slow standard retrieve. Patterns associated with dragonfly nymphs are: Carey Special; Dragonfly Nymph (dark green and brown); Woolly Buggers.

FORAGE FISH

Small fish which are born in the spring in the shallows of the lake often become easy prey for larger fish. They are 1/4-2 inches in length and their color varies depending on the specific species found in a lake. Minnows swim close to the shore around vegetation, logs and rocks, seeking their own food. Imitations should be fished both in shallows and deeper water along the shoreline next to drop offs. To simulate a swimming minnow use short fast strips and twitches, alternated with pauses. The strip tease can also add to the enticing erratic movement of the fly. Patterns associated with forage fish are: Stayner Ducktail, Spruce Fly, Muddler Minnow, Zonker.

LEECHES

Leeches are flat worms with suckers at each end and they are found in many lakes. They become a supplemental trout food source when insects are not plentiful. Leeches average 1-2 inches in length; however, they often appear longer when they are swimming and may be up to 4 inches in length. They may be gray, brown, red or black in color. Leeches are found at various depths around vegetation and bottom debris. They are best fished when there is little sunlight, early and late and on windy, cloudy

This cutthroat trout has taken an artificial fly that is tied to simulate its natural food source.

days. They swim with a slow undulating snake like motion, but can move faster if threatened. The leech is fished at all depths with a standard or hand twist retrieve. A leech pattern is also a good fly to use when searching for fish. Patterns associated with leeches are: Canadian Brown Leech; Mohair Marabou Leech, Woolly Buggers and Woolly Worms in black, maroon, purple, brown, grey; Beaver and Tan Leech; and Halloween Leech.

SCUD

Scud (often referred to as shrimp) are one species of crustacean that is prevalent in all lakes, particularly where the water has high alkalinity and oxygenation. They are a major food source for trout all year long. Scud resemble insects in that they have jointed appendages but have no heads and they mate and develop in the water, rather than through hatching. They breathe through abdominal gills and their bodies are usually encased in a hard layer. Scud grow from 1/4 to 1/2 inches in length and range in color from grey, olive/grey to tannish pink. They live in shallow vegetated areas and in bottom debris where they look for food by crawling or swimming backward. Although scud may appear to have a curled shape when you observe them on land, they are tied on straight hooks because their bodies straighten out when they move. When fishing scud, cast toward weeds and let your fly sink right into the weeds, lift your rod and jiggle it, then lower it into weeds again. Also use a very slow retrieve, keeping your fly on or near the bottom and alternate with erratic/jerky movements followed by a pause. Patterns associated with scud are: Scud; Shellback Shrimp.

SUMMARY

Now you have been introduced to the trout food that you must imitate in order to catch trout: what it looks like, what life stage is the most significant for trout fishing; how these aquatic animals move; when they are most likely to be of interest to trout; and how to fish each kind of aquatic animal. The next chapter describes in detail how each of the basic artificial lake flies is constructed so that you can identify it in a fly fishing shop or tie one yourself.

Leeches provide supplemental trout food when aquatic insects are not available. Leeches can be found at all depths and are best fished when there is minimal sunlight or on windy days.

CHAPTER 6

ARTIFICIAL LAKE FLY PATTERNS

ORIENTATION

Most of the artificial fly patterns described in this chapter are listed under various categories of trout food in the previous chapter. However, a few patterns described in this chapter are not usually associated with a particular species. They are included because they have proven to be effective lake flies.

You will also note that a particular fly pattern may have been listed under several categories of trout food. The reason for this is that most of the flies are not true imitations, but are more "suggestive" of the food source. By varying the size, color and bulkiness of an artificial it can suggest different species of insect. For example, the Carey Special, when tied on a large hook with heavy hackle, can suggest a dragon fly nymph and when tied on a smaller hook and sparse hackle can suggest a damsel or caddis. When selecting sizes of artificials that imitate or suggest an insect, also remember that as the season progresses, select smaller flies.

Dave Hughes (1993) suggests that stillwater fly fishers, particularly those who also stream fish, should set up separate fly boxes to store their basic lake flies. The boxes can be labeled and organized around the various trout food groupings: e.g. leeches and scuds, dragon and damsel nymphs. With this type of organization it becomes easier to find the flies needed at a particular time and also to separate lake fly boxes from stream fly boxes.

The fly patterns in this chapter are listed alphabetically and in addition to regular directions for tying, there are special instructions where appropriate. A general rule to follow, however, is that the less dressing of the fly the better, especially in clear water. Hackle and body materials are more effective when tied sparsely. Some directions call for tying the hackle "inside out". This means that the hackle is tied on before the body thus making for a more sparcely tied fly. Appendix V provides a detailed description of the hooks that are used to tie lake flies.

For those of you who choose not to tie your own flies or because of physical limitations cannot, these descriptive patterns will help you to select effective lake flies from an outfitter or fly shop. If a fly shop does not carry the flies you need, they may be willing to tie them for you. Or if you are lucky, you just might find a fellow fly fisher who is willing to make them for you.

LAKE FLY PATTERNS

BIGGS FLY (SHEEP CREEK)

Hook: 6-16, 1X-4X long
Thread: Black
Tail: Three turns of brown hackle flared at bend of hook. Hackle just wider than the hook gap. Should be fairly sparse
Body: Fine dark olive green chenille wrapped as tightly as possible
Wing: Mallard flank (about 20 fibers), when tied in at head reaches just short of the hackled tail over the top of the hook
Variations: Keeping same proportions, use different colored chenille, peacock herl, fine silver tinsel rib
Note: Developed by George Biggs of Jerome, Idaho.

BEAVER AND TAN LEECH

Hook: 8-12 3X-4X long
Thread: Black
Tail: Clump of black or brown marabou no longer than the hook shank
Body: Variegated medium dark brown and tan chenille
Hackle: Brown or black palmered. Tied "inside out" (before the chenille) and clipped to 1/4 in length

CALLIBAETIS NYMPH

Hook: 12-16 1X long
Thread: Black or olive
Tail: Dyed olive brown partridge or grouse fibers
Rib: Fine copper wire
Body: Abdomen and thorax, mottled light olive brown blend dubbing. Pick out thorax for legs
Wingcase: Ringneck pheasant tail fibers pulled over thorax
Variations: Flashback made with flat silver tinsel for wingcase as developed by Tim Tollett of Dillon, Montana.

CANADIAN BROWN LEECH

Hook: 6-10 3X-4X long
Thread: Black
Body: Canadian brown mohair with fibers picked out in shape of a leech

The fly tyer needs a comfortable, well lighted place for the hours that she or he may spend in the creative activity of fly tying. The five basic tools for fly tying are: vice with adjustable jaws for holding the hooks; sharp scissors with fine points for trimming thread; bobbin to hold the thread under tension; hackle pliers for wrapping hackle; and a bodkin (needle) to apply head cement. Other materials used include: hooks, threads, body material, hackles, wings and tails, head cement, wax and finishing tool.

Variations: Black, red mohair body. Tails of brown or black marabou or with a few strands of Flashabou.

CAREY SPECIAL

Hook: 4-14 3X-4X long
Thread: Black
Tail: Optional. A few strands of ringneck pheasant rump fibers, 3/4 inch long
Body: fine dark olive chenille
Hackle: Ring neck pheasant rump feathers tied in at head, around the body and extending past the bend of the hook
Variations: Body can be tied with peacock herl, dubbing or floss in various shades of green. To simulate a dragon fly nymph use heavier hackle and for damsel fly nymphs sparse hackle.

DAMSELFLY NYMPH

Hook: 8-12 3X-4X long
Thread: Olive
Tail: Stubby light olive marabou (marabou should always be carefully torn not clipped)
Body and Thorax: Fine olive chenille
Hackle: Olive hackle palmered over thorax, clipped to 1/4 inch on sides and bottom
Variations: Tie body and thorax with olive or insect green yarn, marabou or chenille; peacock herl

DRAGONFLY NYMPH

Hook: 6-12 4X long
Thread: Olive
Tail: Dark olive marabou (short)

Body: Large size dark olive green chenille
Thorax: Medium/small size dark olive green chenille
Wingcase: Bunch of pheasant tail fibers tied between body and head over the thorax
Hackle: Dark olive green grizzly hackle, 3 wraps between body and head, clipped top and bottom
Variations: Body may be tied with dark olive marabou or yarn

GRIFFITH'S GNAT

Hook: 16-28 3X fine
Thread: Black
Body: Peacock herl
Hackle: Palmered grizzly, can be trimmed top and bottom so that the fly floats flush with the surface film
Note: Developed by George Griffith.

HALF BACK

Hook: 8-12 1X-4X long
Thread: Black
Tail: A few pheasant tail fibers
Body: Fine dark olive green chenille
Thorax: Continuation of body material
Wingcase: Pheasant tail fibers tied in between body and thorax and at head
Hackle: The ends of the wingcase fibers are folded back and tied beard style
Variations: Different colors green and brown chenille for body/thorax. Full back style, tie wingcase in at tail, extending over body and tied in at head

ARTIFICIAL LAKE FLY PATTERNS

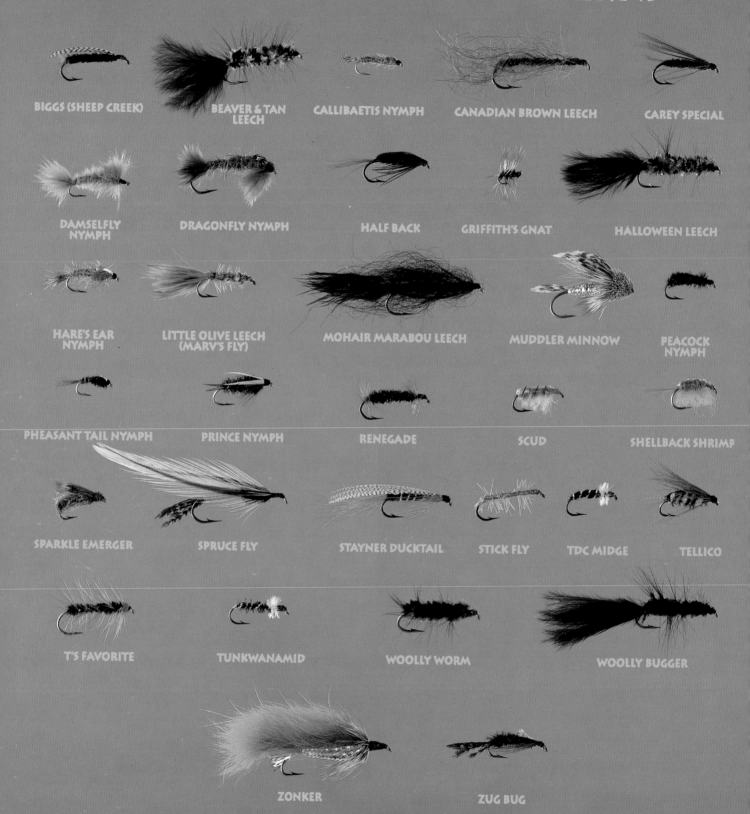

BIGGS (SHEEP CREEK)

BEAVER & TAN LEECH

CALLIBAETIS NYMPH

CANADIAN BROWN LEECH

CAREY SPECIAL

DAMSELFLY NYMPH

DRAGONFLY NYMPH

HALF BACK

GRIFFITH'S GNAT

HALLOWEEN LEECH

HARE'S EAR NYMPH

LITTLE OLIVE LEECH (MARV'S FLY)

MOHAIR MARABOU LEECH

MUDDLER MINNOW

PEACOCK NYMPH

PHEASANT TAIL NYMPH

PRINCE NYMPH

RENEGADE

SCUD

SHELLBACK SHRIMP

SPARKLE EMERGER

SPRUCE FLY

STAYNER DUCKTAIL

STICK FLY

TDC MIDGE

TELLICO

T'S FAVORITE

TUNKWANAMID

WOOLLY WORM

WOOLLY BUGGER

ZONKER

ZUG BUG

Jim Schollmeyer photo

HALLOWEEN LEECH

Hook: 8-12 3X-4X long
Thread: Black
Tail: Brown or black marabou, 1/3 of the length of body
Body: Fine/medium orange and black variegated chenille, also with crystal
Hackle: Brown or black tied "inside out"

HARE'S EAR NYMPH

Hook: 12-18 1X long
Thread: Black
Tail: Tuft of natural hare's ear mask
Rib: 16/18 pearl or flat gold tinsel or fine copper wire
Body: Abdomen and thorax light or dark hare's ear or mixed. Pick out thorax to make shaggier
Wingcase: Mottled turkey or pheasant tail
Variations: For flash back use flat silver tinsel for wing case as developed by Tim Tollett, of Dillon, Montana. May also be tied without rib

LITTLE OLIVE LEECH (MARV'S FLY)

Hook: 8-12 3X long
Thread: Olive (to match hackle)
Tail: Olive marabou (to match hackle) the length of hook shank
Body: Olive/gold variegated chenille (fine and tied very slim)
Rib: Olive hackle palmered over the chenille body. Trim short all around
Note: Developed by Marvin Taylor, Boise, Idaho. Taylor uses grizzly saddle hackle dyed with #42 golden/yellow Rit dye.

MOHAIR AND MARABOU LEECH

Hook: 2-14 3X-4X long
Thread: Black
Tail: Brown marabou the length of shank
Body: One layer of Canadian Brown mohair yarn secured in at rear of hook and wrapped forward. As you wind, pull fibers toward back of hook thus developing a leech shape. Pick out more fibers if more shagginess is desired
Variations: Black, Canadian Blood and purple mohair and marabou

MUDDLER MINNOW

Hook: 10-12 1-2X long
Thread: Brown
Tail: Mottled turkey quill
Body: Flat gold tinsel
Underwing: Gray squirrel tail
Overwing: Mottled turkey quill
Hackle: Deer hair, tied in a collar
Head: Deer hair, spun and clipped

PEACOCK NYMPH

Hook: 10-16 regular
Thread: Black
Body: Peacock herl
Collar: Black ostrich herl
Legs: Black hackle fibers tied at head beard style

PHEASANT TAIL NYMPH

Hook: 10-16 regular
Thread: Brown
Tail: Ringneck pheasant center tail fibers

Rib: Fine gold wire
Body: Ringneck pheasant center tail fibers
Legs: Ringneck pheasant center tail fiber tips
Variations: Flashback tied with flat silver tinsel for wing case as developed by Tim Tollett, Dillon, Montana. May also be tied without rib

PRINCE NYMPH

Hook: 8-16 regular or 1X long
Thread: Black
Tail: Two brown goose biots tied in a V, 1/2 of body length
Body: Peacock herl
Rib: Size 16/18 gold mylar tinsel
Hackle: Brown tied beard style
Wings: Two white goose biots, one on each side, the length of the hook shank

RENEGADE

Hook: 10-16 1X long
Thread: Black
Body: Peacock herl (thin body)
Hackle: Rear and front, 2 turns of brown hackle, flared
Variations: Rib of silver tinsel and red thread tied at tag and head

SCUD

Hook: 8-14 regular or 2X short
Thread: Olive
Tail: Olive fibers (short)
Body: Olive dubbing
Shellback: Narrow strip of clear plastic cut from freezer bag
Rib: Silver wire, clear monofilament or Krystal Flash

SHELLBACK SHRIMP

Hook: 8-14 regular
Thread: Olive
Body: Olive gray dubbing
Shellback: Narrow plastic strip
Rib: Monofilament or silver wire

SPARKLE EMERGER

Hook: 12-18 2-3X fine
Thread: Olive
Underbody: Olive sparkle yarn
Overbody: Olive sparkle yarn
Wing: Light brown deer hair
Variations: For body use different colors of sparkle yarn
Note: Developed by Gary LaFontaine.

SPRUCE FLY

Hook: 2-10 3X long
Thread: Black
Tail: Peacock sword
Body: Rear half red floss, front half peacock herl
Wing: Two light badger saddle hackles tied back to back and on edge, extended to end of the tail
Hackle: Three turns of light badger hackle
Variations: Dark badger wings and hackle

STAYNER DUCKTAIL

Hook: 6-12 3X-4X long
Thread: Black

Tail: Bright orange hackle fibers
Body: Fine/medium dark olive chenille
Rib: Fine embossed gold tinsel
Hackle: Bright orange hackle fibers tied beard style
Wing: Mallard flank feather tied flat on top of body, to reach end of tail
Variations: May be tied with different colored bodies and variegated chenille
Note: Developed by Ruel Stayner of Jerome, Idaho.

STICK FLY

Hook: 8-12 2-3X long
Thread: Olive
Body: Olive colored floss
Hackle: Olive palmered, trimmed to 1/4 inch
Variations: Various shades of floss and with fine olive chenille. This fly should be very slim and stick-like.

T'S FAVORITE

Hook: 10-16 2X-3X long
Thread: Black
Body: Peacock herl
Rib: Fine gold wire
Hackle: Brown palmered. Tie off with three turns of wire. Spiral wire forward toward the head
Head: 1/8 inch of red dubbing
Note: Developed by Tim Tollett, Dillon, Montana.

TDC MIDGE

Hook: 10-16 regular and 2X long
Thread: Black
Body: Black wool yarn with rib of fine silver tinsel
Thorax: Black chenille, should look thick
Collar: Several turns of white ostrich herl

A typical morning launching site at a large Montana lake.

TELLICO

Hook sizes: 6-16 1X long
Thread: Black
Tail: Guinea feather fibers
Shellback: Ringneck pheasant center tail fibers or dash of turkey brown
Rib: Peacock herl
Body: Yellow fur or synthetic yarn
Hackle: Two turns of brown hen beard style

TUNKWANAMID

Hook: 10-16 3-4X long
Thread: Black
Tag: Fine silver tinsel
Body: One poor quality strand of peacock herl
Rib: Fine silver tinsel
Head: White ostrich herl, 4-5 turns

WOOLLY WORM

Hook: 2-16 2X-4X long
Thread: Black
Body: Any color medium chenille or peacock herl
Hackle: Palmered grizzly, black or brown hackle. For more sparse hackle tie "inside out"

Author with large rainbow caught with a small Tunkwanamid fly, fished slowly during a chironomid hatch on Mission Lake.

WOOLLY BUGGER

Hook: 2-10 3X long
Thread: Black
Tail: Black marabou 3/4 of the length of body
Body: Medium black chenille
Hackle: Black palmered "inside out"
Variations: Olive, green and purple chenille and marabou; crystal chenille body. Tied with either olive or brown hackle. For sparse hackle tie inside out

ZONKER

Hook: 2-3 2X long
Thread: Black
Body: Mylar piping
Wing: Rabbit fur strip
Hackle: Grizzly
Butt: Red thread, used to tie down both wing and body

ZUG BUG

Hook: 6-16 1X long
Thread: Black
Tail: Peacock sword
Rib: Oval silver tinsel
Body: Peacock herl
Hackle: Brown hen beard style, sparse
Wingcase: Woodduck flank, clipped short

BIBLIOGRAPHY

REFERENCES

Alley, Robert, "Float Tube Strategy." *Trout,* pp 46-49, Spring 1992.

Borger, Gary, *Stillwater Fly Fishing,* Gary Borger Enterprises, Wassau, WI.

Cordes, Ron & Randall Kaufmann, *Lake Fishing with a Fly,* Frank Amato Publications, Portland, Oregon, 1984.

Farrow, Brian, "Float Tube Kick-Twitch-and Stop." *Fly Fisherman,* pp 54-55, February 1994.

Hughes, Dave, "A Lake Fly Box.", *Flyfishing,* pp 23-26, Nov-Dec 1993.

Taylor, Marvin, *Float Tubes and Fly Rods,* Claxton Printers, Caldwell, Idaho, 1979.

Taylor, Marvin, *Float Tubing the West,* Belly Boat Publishing, Boise, Idaho, 1994.

Trump, Gene, "Float Tube Tactics." *Fly Fisherman,* pp 52-55, February 1994.

Whitlock, Dave, "Float Tube Basics." *American Angler,* pp 21-24, March/April 1992.

RESOURCES

ARTICLES

Alley, Robert, "Float Tube Strategy." *Trout,* pp 46-49, Spring 1992.

Beck, Cathy and Barry, "Fly Tying Tools: The Basics." *Flyfishing,* pp 28-29, February 1994.

Fong, Michael, "Secrets of the Summer Pond." *Fly Fisherman,* pp 34-36, 67-68, Summer 1992.

Probasco, Steve, "Chironomids." *Flyfishing,* pp 72 & 63, February 1994.

BOOKS

Alley, Robert, *Advanced Lake Fly Fishing,* Frank Amato Publications, Portland, Oregon, 1991.

Andreasen, Mike & Allan Ryther, *Effective Lake Flies,* ALLAMI Publications, West Jordan, Utah, 1990.

Chan, Brian M, *Flyfishing Strategies for Stillwaters,* Frank Amato Publications, Portland, Oregon, 1991.

Cordes, Ron & Randall Kaufmann, *Lake Fishing with a Fly,* Frank Amato Publications, Portland, Oregon, 1984.

Davy, Alfred G. (ed), *The Gilly—A Flyfisher's Guide,* Frank Amato Publications, Portland, Oregon, 1991.

Dirksen, D. J. & R. A. Reeves, *Recreation Lakes of California,* Recreation Sales Publishing, P.O. Box 4024, Burbank, California 91503-4024.

Hughes, Dave, *Strategies for Stillwater,* Stackpole Publishing, Harrisburg, Pennsylvania, 1991.

Hughes, Dave, *American Fly Tying Manual,* Frank Amato Publications, Portland, Oregon, 1986.

Meyer, Deke, *Float Tube Fly Fishing,* Frank Amato Publications, Portland, Oregon, 1989.

Scheiss, Bill, *Fishing Henry's Lake,* Pioneer Press, Mountain Home, Idaho, 1988.

VIDEOTAPES

Borger, Gary, "Stillwater Fly Fishing," Gary Borger Enterprises, P.O. Box 628, Wausau, WI 54402-0628.

Krieger, Mel, "The Essence of Fly Casting," 790 27th Ave., San Francisco, California 94121.

JOURNALS

Flyfishing: Publisher, Frank Amato; Editor, Marty Sherman.

Fly Rod & Reel: Publisher, Down East Enterprise, Inc.; Editor, Silvio Calabi.

American Angler: Publisher, Joe Migliore; Editor, Jack Russell.

Fly Fisherman: Publisher and Editor, John Randolph.

Trout: Publisher, Trout Unlimited; Editor, Peter A. Rafle, Jr.

CATALOGS

Cabela's, Spring Fly Fishing Edition, 812 13th Ave., Sidney, Nebraska, 69160.

Frontier Anglers, 680 N. Montana St., Dillon, Montana 59725.

Kaufmann's Streamborn, P.O. Box 23032, Portland, Oregon, 97223.

LL Bean, Fly Fishing Edition, Freeport, Maine 04033.

Mike's Fly Desk, Float Tubing Specialists, 2395 S. 150th St., Bountiful, Utah, 84010.

Orvis, Spring Fishing Edition, P.O. Box 798, Manchester, Vermont, 05254-0798.

The Fly Shop, 4140 Churn Creek Rd., Redding, California 96002.

ORGANIZATIONS

Trout Unlimited, 1500 Wilson Blvd., Arlington, Virginia 22209. This is a national conservation organization with both state and local chapters. Membership in this organization will help you find out more about fishing habitats, advocacy for trout waters and can put you in touch with other fly fishers and fly fishing clubs.

Federation of Fly Fishermen, P.O. Box 1595, Bozeman, Montana 59758.

National Wildlife Federation, 8925 Leesberg Pike, Vienna, Virginia 22180.

Nature Conservancy, 1800 N. Kent St., Arlington, Virginia, 22209.

Henry's Lake Foundation, 7545 Southside Blvd., Nampa, Idaho 83686.

Golden West Women Flyfishers, P.O. Box 22068, San Francisco, California 94122.

APPENDIX I

SINK RATES AND RECOMMENDED DEPTHS FOR SELECTED SINKING LINES

	Sink Rate Inches per Second	Recommended Depth in Feet
Scientific Angler		
Intermediate	1.25-1.75	3-5
Wet Cel I	1.75-2.50	5-10
Wet Cel II	2.00-3.00	10-20
Wet Cel III	3.25-4.25	20-30
Wet Cel IV	3.75-6.25	30-40
Cortland		
Type I	1.25-1.50	5-10
Type II	1.50-2.50	10-20
Type III	3.50-4.00	20-30
Type IV	4.25-5.00	30-40

APPENDIX II

HOW TO RIG LINES

Author's note: If all this seems too much for you to learn in the beginning, take your gear to a fly shop. Most will be happy to show you how it is done. However, you will want to learn to be particularly skilled in tying your leader to your fly line and your fly to your leader to assure that you won't lose a fish through a faulty knot.

ATTACHING BACKING TO FLY LINE

In order to know how much backing to use on the reel, first attach the fly line to the backing so that you can wind both lines on the spool. Unwind 2-3 feet of line from the spool it comes on and attach the fly line to the backing using a nail knot.

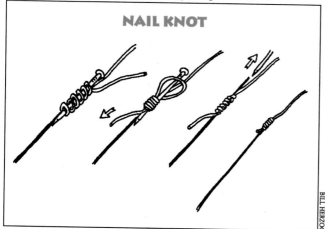

NAIL KNOT

BILL HERZOG

◆ Directions for nail knot:
    a. Place a small nail or nail knot tool under the fly line and hold with the thumb and forefinger of the left hand. Leave about 1/2 inch of the line and nail

sticking out from between your fingers. Place the end of the butt section of the leader under the nail/tool, leaving about four inches to wrap.
    b. With your right hand, make five loose wraps with the butt section of the leader over the nail working toward the tip of the line. With the thumb and forefinger of the left hand, loosely hold the five wraps so they don't unwind and work the end of the butt section under the wraps alongside the nail.
    c. Tighten the knot by pulling gently on the butt section and leader. Slide the nail out while still holding the wraps with your fingers and tighten again to take up the slack.
    d. Make sure that all the wraps are symmetrical before final tightening. Pull on the leader and butt section to tighten. Trim the tag ends.

Once the fly line and backing are attached begin to wind the fly line onto the reel followed by the backing. When the backing reaches 3/16th of an inch from the outside of the rim of the spool, that is enough backing. Carefully remove backing and line from the reel and prepare to attach the backing to the reel spool.

ATTACHING BACKING TO REEL SPOOL

The arbor knot is the best knot for attaching the backing to the reel spool.

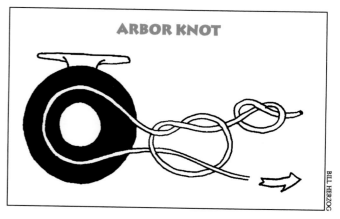

ARBOR KNOT

BILL HERZOG

◆ Directions for arbor knot:
    a. After threading the end of the backing around the arbor (the round shaft joining the two sides of the reel), the backing will be in two parallel lines. Tie an overhand knot in the short line and tighten it.
    b. Then take that knotted end of the short line and make another overhand knot around the long line that goes to the backing spool. Draw that tight.
    c. Next take the long line above the knot and slowly pull until both knots are snugged against each other on the arbor. Trim the tag end.
    d. Attach the reel to the rod to make winding the backing and fly line easier. Make tight, smooth layers as you wind on the lines.

ATTACHING LEADER TO FLY LINE

Use any one of these three methods to attach leader to fly line:
1. Nail knot.
2. Slip on leader loop (Cortland, $4.50 for 4) can be attached to the end of the fly line using the directions on the package.

LOOP KNOT

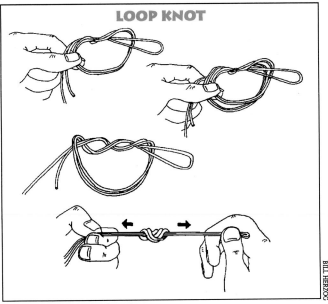

BILL HERZOG

◆ Directions clinch knot:
   a. Thread the leader through the eye of the hook, leaving a 4-6 inch tag end. Make 5 turns with the tag end around leader.

CLINCH KNOT

BILL HERZOG

   b. There is a small loop in the leader just above the eye of the hook. Thread the tag end through this loop. Now you have formed a loop with the leader. Run the tag end through this loop, wet the knot and, while holding the tag end and hook securely in your left hand, pull the leader slowly away from the hook and snug the knot against the eye. Trim the tag end.

   Note: To further strengthen the clinch knot, after step (a) tie an overhand knot at the end of the tag end and when you pull the tag end down toward the eye pull this knot right into the clinch knot.

ATTACHING THE FLY TO LEADER

Use any one of these three knots:
1. Clinch knot
2. Loop knot: This knot is used with smaller flies tied onto heavy leader material. The loop should be 1/4-1/2 inches.
3. Turle knot: This knot is useful for large flies and leaders.

◆ Directions for loop knot:
   a. Double the end of the leader to form a loop and tie an overhand knot at the base of the double line.
   b. Leave loop open in knot and bring doubled line through once more.
   c. Hold leader and tag end and pull loop to tighten knot. Size of loop can be determined by pulling loose knot to desired point and holding it while knot is tightened.
   d. With loops in both fly line and leader, pass the leader loop through the line loop. Pass the small end of the line loop through the leader loop and tighten by pulling in opposite directions.
3. No-knot eyelet. (Purchase no-knot eyelet in smallest size, package of 15 for less than $3) The shaft of the eyelet has a barbed portion which you slide into the end of the fly line.

NO-KNOT EYELET

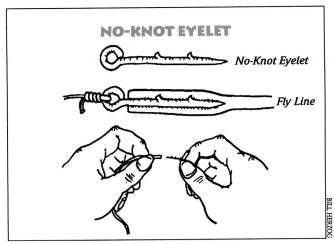

No-Knot Eyelet

Fly Line

BILL HERZOG

TURLE KNOT

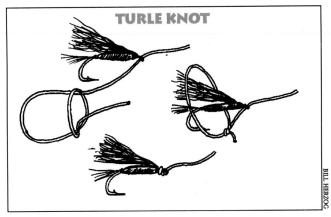

BILL HERZOG

◆ Directions for no-knot eyelet:
   a. Using a small sized needle open a hole in the end of the line by pushing the needle as far as you can into the end of the fly line. Then using pliers to assist, push the serrated no-knot eyelet into the end of the fly line until just the loop is exposed. Seal around the head of the line with pliobond and let dry.
      3a. Clinch Knot. Tie the leader into the eye of the no-knot eyelet with a clinch knot.

◆ Directions for turle knot:
   a. Pass the end of the leader through the eye of the hook and form a 3 inch loop with a slip knot.
   b. Pull the loop back over the fly. While holding the knot against the eye of the hook with your thumb and fore finger of your left hand.
   c. Snug the knot tight with your right hand. Trim the tag end of the leader.

APPENDIX III

POWER ASSISTED TUBING

The availability of the POW-R Tube™ system to serious float tube fly fishing men and women is a tremendous advantage for those who have diminished physical ability due to age or disability as well as those venturing on wide and windy waters. The POW-R Tube™ allows you to continue fishing effectively when your body imposes limitations and when safety concerns are paramount.

The POW-R ™ set-up has two tubes. The main tube is an oversized wedge shape in which the fly fisher sits. The smaller tube holds the deep-cell marine battery and is connected to the main tube by a zipper.

DEVELOPMENT

The initial prototypes of this electrically-powered tube were begun in 1984 at Yellowstone Wilderness Supply located in West Yellowstone, Montana, by the recently deceased Bill Akers and patented by him prior to his death. From the beginning the POW-R Tube™ has gone through extensive testing and modifications. Some of the greats of float tube fly fishing have been involved in this development: George Biggs originator of the Sheep Creek Fly; Ruel Stayner originator of the Stayner Ducktail; Marvin Taylor, fishing writer; and John and Pat O'Neall who have fished the western waters for close to 30 years. These serious, knowledgeable tube fishers each contributed his or her expertise to developing and improving this innovation in float tube fly fishing.

What the current model allows you to do is move both forward and backward without strenuous kicking and, contrary to many other kinds of boats, leaves both your hands free for fish-

The control switch is easily reached on the main tube. Wires lead from this control unit to the battery and motor.

The unit is assembled by: placing the motor on its mount; moving the tube into water deep enough to accommodate the propeller shaft; placing the battery in the small tube battery box; connecting the leads; and finally, checking the controls for proper functioning.

ing. Also fish are seldom spooked by the POW-R Tube™ as they often are by other motor-powered boats.

DESCRIPTION

The main tube is an oversized wedge shape which provides more comfort and stability for the fly fisher. A smaller tube which contains the power unit is attached by a zipper, so that the whole unit can be easily separated for storage and transport. A single power control switch is mounted on the main tube with easy access for manual control which does not interfere with casting or other fishing activity. Wires lead from the control unit to positive and negative poles on a 12-volt marine battery, which fits in a deep specially designed tub in the smaller tube. Another lead goes from the control to a 17 pound thrust Minn-Kota motor which is mounted on the rear of the power unit. The motor moves the tube four speeds backward and two speeds forward. Since most fly fishing from a tube with sinking lines is in the rearward direction, there are more options for going backward. The motor is designed to run straight and for easy and effective turning by using your fins in the direction you want to move. Batteries are re-charged each night, after fishing, with battery chargers plugged into normal AC outlets and the charge lasts for a full day of fishing, even in adverse conditions.

In 1988, the POW-R Pac was developed because of the demand of many tube owners who wanted to add power to their conventional tubes. The POW-R Pac is designed to attach to any existing tube. It has the same power tube unit, but instead of a zipper attachment, it has straps to attach it to the main tube. This unit provides the tube owner with the advantages of the POW-R Tube™ without having to invest in another basic tube.

ADVANTAGES AND STRATEGIES

The addition of power to your tube immediately opens up the opportunity to cover more water in search of fish on big lakes without the strain of strenuous kicking and with the assurance that if a heavy wind does come up you will be able to return to your launching site quite readily. This power unit adds years to your ability to continue float tube fly fishing.

As described in Chapter 3 on methods, a strategy to use when searching for fish or for enticing fish to take your fly is to alter the speed that you kick as well as the speed of the retrieve. Although most of the time fishing is done on the slowest speed, with the POW-R Tube™ you can easily increase the speed that your fly travels simply by turning up the controls. The fast 3-4 speed is often just the thing to turn on the fish when nothing else seems to stimulate them. And, the trolling method becomes a real joy with the motor propelling you along and the fly drifting behind. You can easily cover more water to locate concentrations of fish. In fact, on warm sunny days one might be even lulled to sleep!

The forward speed also has its unique contribution to fishing success. When a heavy, strong fish is on your line, it might take you right to the end of the backing line with nothing else to give the fish in its desire to escape you. By switching to your forward speed, you can follow the fish without risking the loss of a fish to a broken leader or hook. The forward speed is also useful when you are fishing to rising fish because it allows you to quietly and easily approach within casting distance of the fish. In addition, the forward direction allows you to approach fish that have taken to the weeds to escape your pursuit. Without this advantage, you have to turn around in order to try to get the fish from the weeds.

The POW-R Tube™ is also helpful in making long casts. As with conventional tubing, you remain stationary when casting, but you can turn on the rear speed to help you pay out more line from your reel or stripping apron. Then you turn the motor off to let it sink to the desired depth and turn it on again to begin your retrieve.

As described in Chapter 3, a windy day is often very productive, especially during the summer doldrums and the winds on western lakes can be most prohibitive to the regular tuber. The tuber with a motor, however, will be able to take full advantage of this fishing bonus and not become exhausted fighting the wind and waves.

CARE OF THE POW-R TUBE™

Because the POW-R Tube™ is based on electrical connections, it is important to understand how the system works in order to problem solve any malfunctions. For example, if the motor becomes tangled in weeds, net or line, it will automatically turn off by breaking the connection through a fuse break, thus preventing damage to the motor. In this case, the motor needs to be disentangled and a fuse replaced. Because of this, you should carry extra fuses in your tube pocket. It is also important to maintain tight connections by keeping all terminals free of rust and debris.

SUMMARY

There is no doubt that the addition of power to your tubing increases your ability to fish a larger surface of water, combat windy conditions, catch bigger and more fish and lessen physical exhaustion.

Resource: Yellowstone Wilderness Supply, P.O. Box 129, 297 Firehole Ave., West Yellowstone, Montana 59715, 800/624-8564 or 406/646-7613.

FLOATING LINE STRATEGIES

There may be times when you choose to use a floating line to fish for trout that are feeding on emerging insects at the sur-face or sub-surface water. For this kind of fishing you can use the same reel/spool combination and the weight forward floating line that is matched for your rod. There are several ways to use the floating line for lake fishing.

CHIRONOMID PUPAE STRATEGIES

Since the chironomid or midge is so abundant in lakes and so vulnerable as it tries to break through the surface film, it is worth rigging for this emergence when it occurs. Using a floating line, coat the leader with greasy line floatant down to the last 12 inches so that it will float, and the tip end will be able to sink down just below the surface where these midge pupa often hang suspended before their final emergence. For this method either no retrieve or an extremely slow hand twist is best. Since the fish are likely to take these insects softly, you need to watch the line very carefully for any movement. If you see movement, simply raise your rod tip and you will know immediately if a fish has taken your fly. You might even consider a line indicator made of colored polypropylene yarn which can be tied into your leader at the end of the greased section as a way to more clearly see when there is movement in your line.

WEIGHTED FLY ON FLOATING LINE

If nymphs, such as *callibaetis,* are emerging and trout are following them to the surface, you can make long casts into the area where the fish are rising using a floating line and weighted nymph. If the trout are cruising, note if they're following a pattern and try to lead your cast ahead of where you expect the fish to swim. When there are many insects to feed on, the trout often feed in a rhythmic pattern that also lets you know when to cast your fly. This method calls for either no retrieve or an extremely slow hand twist retrieve.

DRY FLY ON FLOATING LINE

There may be other times when trout are cruising along the shoreline taking adult insects from the surface. You might choose to try this type of sighted fishing rather than that done with the intermediate or sinking line. Again try to pick up patterns of feeding and movement to be able to anticipate when and where the trout will be and when you expect it to feed.

HOOKS FOR TYING ARTIFICIAL FLIES

Two major brands of hooks used for tying these flies are Mustad or Tiemco (TM). Each has strong tensile quality, a separate number to identify the length of the hook shank and type of hook and each has a variety of hooks and sizes. The length and type of hooks most often used for tying lake flies are:

- Regular = Mustad 3906 or TM 3769
- 1X long = Mustad 3906B or TM3761
- 2X long = Mustad 9671 or TM 5262
- 3X long = Mustad 9672 or TM5263
- 4X long = Mustad 9673 or TM 5264
- 3X fine = Mustad 94833 or TM 5230

LEARN MORE ABOUT FLY FISHING AND FLY TYING WITH THESE BOOKS

If you are unable to find the books shown below at your local book store
or fly shop you can order direct from the publisher below.

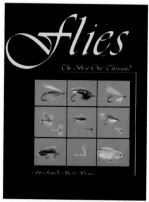

Flies: The Best One Thousand
Randy Stetzer
$24.95

Fly Tying Made Clear and Simple
Skip Morris
$19.95 (HB: $29.95)

The Art of Tying the Dry Fly
Skip Morris
$29.95 (HB:$39.95)

Curtis Creek Manifesto
Sheridan Anderson
$7.95

American Fly Tying Manual
Dave Hughes
$9.95

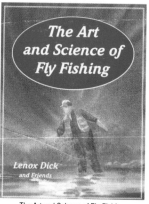

The Art and Science of Fly Fishing
Lenox Dick
$19.95

Western Hatches
Dave Hughes, Rick Hafele
$24.95

Lake Fishing with a Fly
Ron Cordes, Randall Kaufmann
$26.95

Advanced Fly Fishing for Steelhead
Deke Meyer
$24.95

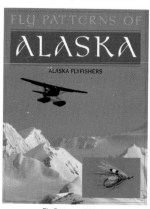

Fly Patterns of Alaska
Alaska Flyfishers
$19.95

Fly Tying & Fishing for Panfish and Bass
Tom Keith
$19.95

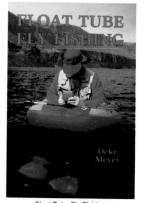

Float Tube Fly Fishing
Deke Meyer
$11.95

VISA, MASTERCARD or AMERICAN EXPRESS ORDERS CALL TOLL FREE: 1-800-541-9498
(9-5 Pacific Standard Time)

Or Send Check or money order to:

Frank Amato Publications
Box 82112
Portland, Oregon 97282

(Please add $3.00 for shipping and handling)